AstroBabe

AstroBabe

A Girl's Guide to the Planetary Powers of Romance

Barrie Dolnick

NEW AMERICAN LIBRARY

New American Library
Published by New American Library, a division of
Penguin Group (USA) Inc., 375 Hudson Street,
New York, New York 10014, U.S.A.
Penguin Books Ltd, 80 Strand,
London WC2R 0RL, England
Penguin Books Australia Ltd, 250 Camberwell Road,
Camberwell, Victoria 3124, Australia
Penguin Books Canada Ltd, 10 Alcorn Avenue,
Toronto, Ontario, Canada M4V 3B2
Penguin Books (NZ), cnr Rosedale and Airborne Roads,
Albany, Auckland 1310, New Zealand

Penguin Books Ltd, Registered Offices:
80 Strand, London WC2R 0RL, England

First published by New American Library,
a division of Penguin Group (USA) Inc.

First Printing, July 2004
10 9 8 7 6 5 4 3 2 1

Ⓟ REGISTERED TRADEMARK—MARCA REGISTRADA

Printed in the United States of America

Book design by Jennifer Ann Daddio

This book is dedicated to

SUSAN STRONG,

the original AstroBabe.

Contents

Preface

It's easy to find advice about your love life—but is it good advice? Your friends will give it to you; chat rooms on the Internet are hotbeds of info; books and magazines and, of course, your mother probably have a lot to say, too. But it's hard to find advice that adds to your wisdom, encourages you to appreciate who *you* are, and helps make romance playful, not painful.

Being an AstroBabe is all that. You'll get to know and love the cool parts of your personality, the hot areas of your passion, and the colorful elements of your mind and heart. You'll appreciate your gifts and you'll manage your less magnetic traits to enjoy romance, flirtation, and love.

You were born with your own personal bundle of charisma, your own preferences for romance and love. *AstroBabe* will help you clearly define these assets by examining your astrological chart. Using only a handful of planets and a simple means to read about them, you'll be able to explore facets of your personal planetary powers to enhance the pleasure of romance. It's easy to find your planets, too. They're only a few clicks away—no fees, no hassles.

An AstroBabe is an informed Babe. She is not a head-in-the-sand or hope-for-the-best type of girl. AstroBabes want to make the most of opportunities to live with exuberance and excitement as well as peace and fulfillment. In other words, AstroBabes take charge of their lives and make them happen.

AstroBabes also know how to evaluate potential suitors and observe how each one contributes differently to a relationship—no two are alike. *AstroBabe* is written for gals with guys in mind. Absorb the information here and you'll make the most of your time with a special guy—and find out how easy it's going to be to stay in sync. There are so many possibilities for your romantic life—be an AstroBabe to find what makes you happiest.

An AstroBabe is a woman who knows herself well. She likes to play with her power (and play nicely, of course) and is comfortable with her vulnerability. She is able to play with love and eventually to stay with love.

AstroBabe: A Girl's Guide to the Planetary Powers of Romance will ignite some of your untapped potential to help you grow into a skillful, playful, and delightful romantic companion.

AstroBabe

ONE

The AstroScoop

Being an AstroBabe requires learning a little bit about the planets through astrology. You do not have to believe in horoscopes. You do not need any special knowledge. All you have to do is let your curiosity lead you through the chapters in this book, read about yourself, and nod, laugh, and shrug at how accurate the stars are in defining what you already know about yourself. You'll also find there are more assets in your planets than you're using now, and, frankly, some liabilities you've been ignoring. This knowledge will guide you to a better way of understanding and enjoying love.

It's all in the stars. Astrology is not just a column

you read in magazines. The study of planets, their motion, and their influence has been around for thousands of years. Ancient civilizations would study the night sky and notice correlations between the moon and its phases, the sun in the constellations, and the planets seen by the naked eye. You would be impressed by the exactness of early astronomers, and astounded by the accuracy of their astrological interpretations. These ancient seers saw the stars more clearly—no big-city lights confounding their view—and they were able to define the constellations, our modern zodiac signs. They saw the Ram of Aries, the Bull of Taurus, the Twins of Gemini, the Crab of Cancer, the Lion of Leo, the Virgin of Virgo, the Scales of Libra, the Scorpion of Scorpio, the Archer of Sagittarius, the Mountain Goat with the Dolphin Tail of Capricorn, the Water Bearer of Aquarius, and the Fish of Pisces. Each of these constellations was a representation of qualities and characteristics that has been handed down through our spiritual ancestors and still rings true today.

Before we get into the planets and their meanings, it's worth mentioning that there is no way to prove exactly how astrology works. Some think the planets have actual vibrations that influence us in our daily lives. Others, like me, consider the planets and their movements simply an uncanny parallel to human reality. In some divine way, they lay a pattern across the sky that foretells, in broad strokes, opportunities, challenges, and events. However mysterious they are, the planets and their movements through the zodiac really do give us a lot of inside information.

Chances are you're familiar with the astrological signs and some of their qualities. You probably know your own sign. Maybe you've read about what signs work well for you and what signs are less compatible. But general astrological information is not enough! You can't use it for targeting specific areas in your life, nor can you consider it very accurate. There are ten heavenly bodies that astrologers call planets, and each one moves at a different pace, through different signs. Horoscopes in magazines look only at the Sun sign. In this book, you will become versed not only in your Sun sign, but your Moon, Mercury, Venus, and Mars. These five planets are your personal planets. Together they form a bundle of charisma that makes you romantic, magnetic, passionate, communicative, approachable, and vulnerable, and provides the many other traits that make you, you.

These five planets offer meaningful and exciting insight into your everyday life and reveal some very personal and powerful qualities you possess. This bundle of planetary energy is called your Personal Planetary Pulse. Here's how it works.

Personal Planetary Pulse

Your Sun sign is a good start—it's the sign of the zodiac that provides you with some basic characteristics and sound gifts you can rely on. Your pulse starts here—but you already know that.

You were also born under a Moon sign. This describes your emotional disposition, unconscious motivations, intuition, mystery, and even sexual energies. You must know your Moon sign to understand your reactions to love and conflict and to help you know the depths of your heart. We'll get into all about how much you like change (or not) and how you can use your Moon sign talents to send psychic messages to the one you want.

Mercury, the planet of communications, is key to making your relationships work. Your Mercury sign will give you an edge on making sure your words are loving, strong, and effective. You'll be able to figure out how best to say what you want to say and not buckle under pressure. Mercury isn't always about words, but also concerns understanding.

Lovely Venus guides you in matters of love—and money—and commitment—if and when it feels right. Venus is the all-purpose love planet and we Astro-Babes use it constantly to flirt, seduce, love, and create the best possible relationship. Your Venus pulse will give you a sense of how much you are willing to do for love and how much you love to love. You may well be surprised.

Fiery Mars, the warrior, pushes you forward (or keeps you to the side) in conflict and passion. Either way, Mars challenges your Venus pulse to be true both to love and to yourself—not always an easy balance. Mars gives fuel to your passion meter. Some people will inspire your love, others simply your "like," and of course there will be some whom you just lust for from Mars' influence.

That's your Personal Planetary Pulse: Sun, Moon, Mercury, Venus, and Mars—a coalition of strengths and gifts that shape your everyday world, your impulses and dreams, your messages and reactions. Imagine knowing how to harness these gifts. You'll be more comfortable in your skin and more capable of navigating your world when you put the best of your planets forward.

Log On and Get Started

How can you find out where your planets are? You don't have to go to an astrologer anymore. You can use one of the many Internet sites that will run your chart without charge—or download free software so that you can run your own.

INTERNET SITES
- astro.com
- alabe.com
- astrology.com
- astrology2go.com

SOFTWARE

- freewarepalm.com (Delphi program)

Reading the Stars

Once you get to a site, you must have personal information on hand, including your birth date (month, day, year), the city in which you were born, and, if possible, the time of your birth. Most sites will give you a chart within seconds. Once you have this on your screen, print it out or write down the sign of each planet. Depending on which site you use, you may receive text that informs you more thoroughly about your planets. If you are unsure about the chart you set, try another site for clarity. I recommend alabe.com for its convenient presentation.

With your chart you'll receive some written analysis and offers for love horoscopes, career horoscopes, etc. These are fine for a brief insight into your life, but won't accomplish what this book will do for you. It's tempting to read the analysis provided by these services. Go ahead. Just don't stop there. Being an AstroBabe is more than learning about the basic planets and signs.

Don't be put off if you see little squiggly symbols on the page. Those are called glyphs and they are just shorthand for the signs and the planets. Here are the signs in shorthand.

♈	Aries
♉	Taurus
♊	Gemini
♋	Cancer
♌	Leo
♍	Virgo
♎	Libra
♏	Scorpio
♐	Sagittarius
♑	Capricorn
♒	Aquarius
♓	Pisces

Each of your planets (Sun, Moon, Mercury, Venus, and Mars) will fall into one of these signs, and the following chapters will give you plenty of insight and advice that can make romance easier and more fulfilling. Forget trying to be like someone else—you can learn to be yourself and love it.

Here's an example. My friend Katerina has the Sun in Capricorn, the Moon in Sagittarius, Mercury in Capricorn, Venus in Scorpio, and Mars in Leo. She was used to reading her horoscope: Capricorns were always about working hard, keeping their nose to the grindstone, being too serious. Then she followed her planets through *AstroBabe*. Sun in Capricorn? Sure, she's ambitious, friendly, serious, and responsible, but that Moon in Sagittarius is all about adventure and fun. Mercury in Capricorn makes her a bit of a worrier, and she chuckled at that one. When she got to Venus in Scorpio and Mars in Leo, she learned about her innate passion, her drive, her sense of fun and playfulness. No way was she a simple Capricorn. She can work when she needs to, but when she plays she's a little fireball: fast, hot, and hard to catch. The right guy for her has both ambition and a thirst for life experience.

Elements and Energies

Signs are the most common currency in astrology and you've probably heard of each one. But now we're going to talk about two more qualities that add another layer of interest and complexity to your chart. Each sign has its own element and modality (which I call energy), which define it even more.

For those of you who are well versed in astrology, this will be familiar territory. If you're new to the subject, read on and enjoy the lightbulbs that go off as you understand more about yourself and others.

ELEMENTS

The elements consist of fire, earth, air, and water. Each sign is ruled by one element. The zodiac starts with a fire sign, Aries, and moves into an earth sign, Taurus. The third sign is air, Gemini, and the fourth is water, Cancer. The elements are then repeated through the zodiac until the last, Pisces.

Fire—Aries, Leo, Sagittarius
Air—Gemini, Libra, Aquarius
Earth—Taurus, Virgo, Capricorn
Water—Cancer, Scorpio, Pisces

These elements give you a feel for how each sign operates. When you understand that you are associated with a certain element, you gain some important self-knowledge. Someone who is a fire sign understands how light and heat are important in life, whereas it's not unusual for water signs to want to live or work near water. (And it's not unusual for fire and water signs to be attracted and repelled by each other at the same time!) Your element tends to be expressed in your life in many ways, and knowing more about it makes you more self-aware and able to satisfy your needs.

Fire

A fire sign operates from passion, aggression, energy, force, movement, initiative, and fearlessness. Fire signs like activity, the art of "doing," learning, moving, traveling, leading, and being "on fire." Look at a flame. You'll see the white-hot tip, where the energy reaches into the air; the yellow heat of the fire that burns and breaks down other elements; the transparent stretch between the yellow and blue flame, where fire's mysterious unseen gas connects spirit to reality; and the cold, blue base where dispassion replaces heat. A fire sign is a complex combination of focus, purpose, and transformation.

Earth

An earth sign is based in reality: practical, tangible, cautious, and patient. Earth favors steadiness, although it is not always still. Consider the earth below your feet. You trust it to support your weight, your house. Earth is not a simple element. We tend to think it's soil, but it can also be deep, sticky mud that can glue you down or slow you up. Earth is also the shifting desert sands, earth in motion. A rockslide or an earthquake is an unpleasant, dangerous shift that occurs when pressures are exerted beyond earth's stability.

People with earth signs can exhibit all of the element's qualities, but most prefer stable, controllable environments. People who have earth planets are very sensitive to the physical world. They like to touch, to sense a presence, to hold love in reality with a hug, a cuddle, a kiss, and maybe a chocolate-chip cookie.

Air

An air sign is about intellect: thought, concepts, communication, strategies. Air signs love to share ideas, consider new angles, create and invent new beliefs. Bliss for an air sign is a meeting of the minds, where being understood and being stimulated intellectually creates a sexy, intriguing bond. Air is light, but it isn't always clear. There are gale-force winds, tornadoes, and pollution that crowd what can be a crisp, clear sky. Foggy thinking and lack of communication are passion killers for air signs. Jousting wit, easy flirtation, or carefully chosen words in a love letter are the best ways to the heart of an air sign.

Water

Water signs are deep—in emotions, imagination, and idealism. Water can exist in three physical mediums: liquid, solid, and gas. Water signs have great depth of feeling, but can shut it off by turning cold, icing solid. Water signs can also expand their emotional spectrum—feeling sad, happy, angry, and hopeful all at once—or go numb when feelings are too much to handle. But water is most comfortable in the state of liquidity, moving through life with its own natural tides, feeling passion, creating fantasy, supporting love with warm, soothing flow. Water signs are complicated, but have the gift of working with all the elements. In air, water is mist; in earth, water enriches and feeds the ground; in fire, it is steam.

The elements express themselves differently in each of the three signs they rule. You will learn more about these elements as you learn about the signs and the planets. You'll also see that your Personal Planetary Pulse is comprised of more than one element. My friend Polly has an earth Sun and Mercury, her Moon and Mars are in fire signs, and her Venus is swimming in water. Polly is not a cut-and-dried earth woman. She has a nice combination of earth, fire, and water to conjure some steamy, sensual passion.

ENERGIES

Elements are not the only extra layer of insight into the planets and their signs. There is also a modality, or energy, associated with each sign: cardinal, fixed, or mutable. You will no doubt recognize yourself when you get there.

Cardinal Energy

Cardinal signs have an energy that is focused on an outcome. They like a task or a challenge and go after a goal with high spirits and excellent prospects. Meet Aries, Cancer, Libra, and Capricorn. Cardinal signs go about their work with dedication and fortitude. Throw something new at them and they'll deal with it. Aries is the fire cardinal sign, who sees a new challenge as a delight. Cancer is the water cardinal sign, who is more cautious about taking on new challenges but gets the job done after careful consideration. Libra is the air cardinal sign; once the situation is fully understood, Libra swiftly targets and strikes the bull's-eye. Capricorn is the earth cardinal sign, and once the challenge has been evaluated for its worthiness, the Capricorn will plan thoroughly and achieve the goal.

Fixed Energy

Fixed signs are not quite so excited about challenges. In fact, fixed signs like the status quo. They take time to make any kind of move, but when they do, it's typically a done deal. Meet Taurus, Leo, Scorpio, and Aquarius. Each one is a study in how not to let anyone tell you what to do. The Taurus, fixed as though planted firmly in earth, is already known for being stubborn. She'll nod and smile and yes you to death but won't make a move without being comfortable with the risk. Leo is the fire version of this, always affable, yet never one to take orders from anyone. Leos are nice about saying no, but say it nonetheless. Scorpio, a passionate water sign, is not as responsive. A Scorpio won't make promises that can't be kept, and won't say yes to something that is not comfortable or safe. A Scorpio stays put until it's painful. But of all fixed signs, the Aquarians have everyone beat. An air sign, Aquarius can float above reality for as long as she likes, never facing a situation that demands movement or change. It's fully within every Aquarian to shift her own life, but she won't always do it, even if the status quo is painful.

Mutable Energy

Last, we have the mutable signs, the shifty, agile signs that can move in any direction. It might seem a refreshing change from those fixed signs, but mutables are very hard to pin down. Gemini, an air sign, is the first mutable sign and Geminis are notoriously changeable. Their attention spans aren't long and many are fairly described as fickle. The great *strength* of mutability is resilience, bouncing back from problems. The hardest thing for Geminis is staying put and forging through the hard times. Virgo is the mutable earth sign, a great sorter of life. Virgos can handle almost any problem and they like it like that. Keep it interesting by giving them something to solve, or they'll shift around until they create something to do. Sagittarius is the sign of fire mutability. Another sign that earns the name "fickle," it's simply interested in so many things that its attention can be short-lived. Passion is what anchors a Sagittarius. Last comes the Pisces, a combination of water and mutability. It's all about imagination, idealism, romance—reality is nowhere near as good. Pisces will be loyal as long as the ideal can be maintained (which, no surprise, takes work).

Here's a summary of the signs, elements, and energies. Notice how each sign is associated with a particular season. You'll see that the cardinal signs always start a new season, the fixed signs are set in only one season, and the mutable signs are transitional, introducing the next season.

Sign	Element	Energy	Season
Aries	Fire	Cardinal	Beginning of spring
Taurus	Earth	Fixed	Spring
Gemini	Air	Mutable	Shift to summer
Cancer	Water	Cardinal	Beginning of summer
Leo	Fire	Fixed	Summer
Virgo	Earth	Mutable	Shift to autumn
Libra	Air	Cardinal	Beginning of autumn

Sign	Element	Energy	Season
Scorpio	Water	Fixed	Autumn
Sagittarius	Fire	Mutable	Shift to winter
Capricorn	Earth	Cardinal	Beginning of winter
Aquarius	Air	Fixed	Winter
Pisces	Water	Mutable	Shift to spring

Bad Stars?

I'm often asked if there's such a thing as a "bad chart" or stars that indicate bad times ahead. There is *no such thing* as a bad chart. Everyone has good times in their stars, and everyone has difficulties as well. It's up to you to use your gifts, to be forgiving of your own weaknesses and those in others. We all have different "assignments" from the universe, and every chart reveals good times and bad. Don't bother to envy someone whose stars seem better than yours. Everyone has what it takes to shine and sparkle in love.

Guys: Compatible, Magnetic, or Downright Disastrous?

Here's where things get interesting. As an AstroBabe, you'll be fully informed about your own power, your own special kind of charisma, charm, and allure. But how will you match up with that guy you really like? Of course, you have to find out where he was born and his birthday. How hard can that be? Then you get to look up his planets just like you did for yourself, and voilà, you have all you need to find your star connections.

You can tell almost immediately where you're going to get along, where the sizzle is, and where the "Oops, I did it again" is going to appear. Your planets, his planets, and a whole lot of interesting stuff is about to happen.

First, you should know about some compulsive, impulsive, and simply-can't-help-it attractions. These range from easy and nice to hot and bothered.

Easy and nice attractions are usually those that involve common elements. Air girls find air guys easy to talk to—so those Gemini, Libra, and Aquarian couples have an easy time at first. Same goes for earth couples, fire couples, and water couples. The downside is that you can be so similar, the relationship may not seem interesting or challenging. You'll find that most magazine horoscopes will tell you that you go best with someone whose Sun sign is in the same element as yours. You know what Astro-Babe says to that? Ho hum. Sure, it can work, but there's a lot more to be said for other combinations.

A Sun-Moon Match

The most favored combination of couples is the girl Moon/boy Sun. That means that your Moon sign is the same as his Sun. That combination is very hakuna matata—no worries! You understand each other.

Compatible and Magnetic Signs

Signs that have an easy connection to you are those that have "compatible" signs with your Sun sign. This in no way limits you to those signs, but you will find that they pop up a lot and that your friends or lovers possess this sign somewhere in their chart. You can find your compatible signs in the next chapter at the end of your Sun sign profile.

Magnetic signs are a different story. Those are usually the "can't keep your hands off them" guys who can and often do lead to trouble. We all have a magnetic sign. After I learned about magnetic signs from my friend and teacher Susan Strong, I looked back and realized many of the great disastrous crushes and relationships of my youth involved just that sign. Susan calls it "the moth to the flame," an attraction so strong you can get hurt from it. You can't help it if you're attracted to him. It does help, however, if there are other signs in your planets or his that get along in a less dramatic way. The passion of a magnetic attraction doesn't last.

A Word About Astrological Guarantees

You might find a guy whose stars are the ultimate match for you: karma, love, passion—everything. But if he's not mature, or if you haven't worked through your own issues, you may not make it. The stars only set you up for a possible long-term union, but you have to do the work yourself. Your karma isn't going anywhere until you face it and deal. That's why even improbable or difficult star combinations can work, too. You have to be a player, a wise, patient, life-affirming, compassionate person, to make the most of all your AstroBabe qualities. You also have to be able to let go of a schmo if he's not going to grow up or be responsible, even if his chart seems tailor-made to mesh with yours.

Personal Planetary Pulse Ratings

To give you a handle on what your unique energy means, AstroBabe includes a rating system from high- to low-intensity signs. Each planet reacts differently with the signs, and what's hot for a Virgo Sun might be cold for a Virgo Moon. Your Personal Planetary Pulse will combine the ratings of each of your five planets into one number. We'll use a scale of 1 to 5, 1 being a low pulse point, more practical than romantic. Higher numbers indicate a rising romantic level. From a look at each planet and its pulse rating, you'll be able to diagnose your own romantic needs and ideals. Don't be surprised if you find that your Personal Planetary Pulse is different than you think.

My friend Gemma, who is a very low-key, soft-spoken woman, never thought of herself as a romantic. Like most women, she hoped for a good relationship, but she didn't go out of her way to meet men. Her Planetary Pulse is

Capricorn Sun	2
Sagittarius Moon	3
Capricorn Mercury	2
Scorpio Venus	3
Leo Mars	4
Total pulse	14

At first Gemma was somewhat surprised that her total pulse indicated that she was a kind of part-time romantic; her personal agenda, career, friends, family, were at least as important as finding the right relationship. But Gemma realized that this was a pretty accurate picture of her, and then wondered about her boyfriend.

Men and AstroBabes

Planets react differently for men and women in each sign. Some signs, like Aries, are more powerfully romantic for men, and other signs, like Pisces, are more strongly romantic for women. When in the next chapter you look at the Planetary Pulse ratings for each sign, you'll see the rating for men beneath the rating for women. This way, once you know his birthday, you can get his chart on the Internet and look up his Planetary Pulse. Then compare it with yours. If he's a mushy romantic and you're a practical, get-it-done girl, you might want to rethink your approach or let him know that you don't go for all those hearts and flowers. It's a great way of avoiding disappointment *and* gives you the advantage of a little insider knowledge of your love object.

Gemma's boyfriend, Mike, had the following planets.

Virgo Sun	3
Capricorn Moon	3
Cancer Mercury	1
Leo Venus	4
Gemini Mars	3
Total pulse	14

To Gemma's delight, Mike's pulse was the same as hers. In other words, they have the same level of romantic interest. They understand the balance between their relationship and the other parts of their lives. Now that Gemma has more insight into their connection, she's enjoying the slow growth of a crush into new love—she's letting herself relax into a natural and easy passion.

AstroBabes Rule

Once you're an AstroBabe, you'll never stop using your insights. You'll remember how earth signs like

to touch, how water signs want to feel trust and passion, that fire signs are go-getters, and that air signs
need to talk and think things through. You'll know
when you're up against a fixed, stubborn guy, a fearless cardinal sign, or that hard-to-pin-down mutable
one. You'll begin to use what you learn here every
day. The more you read about the qualities of each
sign and each planet, the more you'll use that knowledge until it becomes second nature.

When you know more about the stars, it's easy
to play lightly with love and flirtation without taking a big risk. You'll be more at ease with yourself,
which makes you all the more attractive to guys.

Love doesn't have to be a faraway ideal or a
what-if fantasy. He can be right here, sitting next to
you, nuzzling your ear. After all, you're an Astro-
Babe. So get going.

TWO

The Sun

Okay, you think you know all about this one. Sure, you've been reading your horoscope since you were eight years old, and you've heard everything there is to hear about your sign. News flash: you haven't, so just sit tight and ready yourself. You'll be getting something new from here on in.

Your Sun is the planet that gives you your basic nature. It stands for your character, your innate motivation, the way you blow through your karma in this lifetime. The Sun is about your individuality, the characteristics you draw on to move about in the world. The Sun is *not* your personality, or what psychologists refer to as your ego, which is governed by your ascendant (see box). Rather, your Sun is the mission you are on to fulfill your destiny in this life.

The Ascendant

The ascendant is the sign that is coming over the horizon at the time of your birth. While examining your ascendant can be useful to understand how you get things done—how you carry out the mission of your Sun sign—this requires knowing your exact time of birth, not available to everyone. If you happen to have your time of birth and notice the ascendant on the printout of your chart, read about the qualities of this sign in its Sun sign profile. It will give you another view into the complex traits that make you a unique AstroBabe.

In most cases, your Sun sign will have you nodding along and saying, "Yeah, that's me," but sometimes it just doesn't fit so well. There are plenty of Leos who are not thrilled with being the center of attention. There are a great number of Capricorns who have a roaring sense of humor. There are even Geminis who don't like to talk, write, and gossip(!). This is because your Sun sign is only one aspect of you. Sure, it's a biggie, but you've got a lot more going on.

Even if you're completely anxious to jump into the mysterious Moon, Mercury, Venus, and Mars aspects of your Planetary Pulse, give a look into your Sun sign and get familiar with the basic energy that governs you. To give a little more spin to your Sun profile, I include there the signs that are compatible—those that are easy to get along with, to like, to understand—and those that are magnetic. Magnetic signs are trouble with a capital T. You'll fall for them time and again and wonder why you keep coming back.

Sun in Aries

ELEMENT: FIRE
ENERGY: CARDINAL

Girls, Aries is quite the little spitfire. You are full of zip, vim, and vigor and have the can-do energy that makes this world an interesting place. Aries rules the ego, the "I," the self. That typically makes you independent, resilient, assertive, fearless, and game for anything. Words you won't hear about yourself? Try "meek," "wuss," "pathetic." Nope, you won't hear anything of the kind.

Think about it. Your element is fire: passionate, hot, consuming. Your energy is cardinal: "Give me a mission and I'll get right on it." Mars, the god of war, is your ruler. Does this make for a very romantic nature?

If the guy is right, it sure does. You have to be motivated, interested, provoked into a relationship. You're not exactly a wilting lily if you don't have a dance partner. You either find one or leave the party. You have the most excellent clarity when it comes to your needs. No guy who is afraid of his own shadow or of your natural ability to hang out and speak your mind is going to make the cut. Insecure guys get very tetchy around Aries girls—you're too together for them. Aries girls can make some guys feel less masculine, which can dim the romance. So what to do if they need to be guys and they want you to be a girl, but your natural strength is overwhelming your femininity? An AstroBabe will find a way to combine her strength with her feminine side. When the balance is there, the combination is irresistible.

Do NOT go all fluffy and flowery just to get a guy. That is a common mistake Aries women make when they want to kick-start romance. Instead of melding softness *and* strength, you might throw your considerable strength into looking ultrafeminine: the clothes, the hair, and the makeup. But the exhilaration of the challenge and the idea that magnetism can be enhanced by outward appearance can lead to that romance killer: a trashy look. Now, if your natural look is GirlBot or Wonder Woman, you don't have to be concerned. But if you're just an ordinary Aries girl, stay away from too much makeup, any leather, too much of anything. Femininity is subtle.

In the early, flirtatious stages, watch your impulse to move things along. Be patient; listen for clues to his interest. Don't let your desire to make it happen get in the way of LETTING it happen. Not every guy needs directions on how to get romantic.

You know you're not all "tough chick." You know that you have a soft place in your heart where you can be silly and sweet and vulnerable. Showing it to someone might be hard because it feels like weakness, but it's not!

Aries AstroBabes ultimately find romance in carefully chosen guys. You can't date for quantity. He's got to be interesting and engaging, fearless and motivated. Keep an eye out for the guys who treat you like an equal. You'll get along beautifully.

AstroBabe Planetary Pulse: 1
Aries Guy Planetary Pulse: 4
Compatible Signs: Leo, Sagittarius, Gemini
Magnetic Sign: Libra

Sun in Taurus

ELEMENT: EARTH
ENERGY: FIXED

Taurus girls don't think they need any tips on romance (but are probably reading this book anyway because heck, who can resist a little nugget or two on the wonder of you?). Frankly, most Taurus women are such naturals at romance that they don't need a lot of tutelage. Unless, of course, they have a history of staying with the wrong guy too long (we'll get to that!).

But let's start with the great stuff. Taurus girls are so sexy. Ruled by Venus, Taurus girls love nature, beauty, luxury, home. They hike; they garden; they can bake; some can even sew. Taurus girls have taste. Taureans like to feel good and have good feelings. The sign is feminine, creative, soft, and steady.

You Taureans don't need to be constantly amused, to be challenged and pushed, questioned and provoked. You like steady Freddies, the guys who are reliable (he called when he said he'd call!) and who aren't big risk takers. Your dream date is happy to eat a great meal and hang out. He is cuddly and touchy and gives good presents.

Taurus girls are earth signs, but that's not to say that you're all earth mothers. Yes, you probably are fertile (be careful!), but you're also stubborn and fixed. Now, let's just think about that, a fixed earth sign. Are you a mountain? A huge boulder? The land you stand on? Whatever you are, honey, you are not exactly movable turf. Contrary to the parable, mountains do not move to Muhammad. Taurus is where the quality of stubbornness was born.

Change is not fun for you. In fact, change is something to be avoided if you can help it. A relationship isn't hard to get; it's hard to leave. Your friends will be knocking their heads against a wall before you decide that maybe you'll consider that you might be unhappy in your relationship. Girl, you can't bake, plant, sew, or decorate yourself a better guy. You have to make it happen by getting out.

It's okay that Taurus girls take their time getting things done. But watch out. Patience can turn into inertia; loyalty can turn into laziness. If you find yourself slowly declining into depression or baking yourself into plus sizes, rethink your romantic strategy.

It might help to remember that you can find someone relatively easily. The way you are, just getting out will open up a world of romance. There are plenty of guys who warm to your natural feminine energy. You only have to be available to them.

AstroBabe Planetary Pulse: 3
Taurus Guy Planetary Pulse: 4
Compatible Signs: Pisces, Scorpio, Cancer
Magnetic Sign: Leo

Sun in Gemini

ELEMENT: AIR
ENERGY: MUTABLE

Gemini AstroBabes, you are the flirts of the stars. Snappy dialogue, sweet praise, impulsive enthusiasm—they are all yours. No one is bored by a Gemini. You are the fresh air in a room full of deadweight. You are the bright mind when others are stuck with dull ideas. You can understand both up and down at the same time. Being mutable, you have the most flexible and agile energy; you can keep track of everyone else and empathize, too.

What's the problem? Boredom. Insecurity. Sarcasm. The darker side of Gemini lies in its own instability. Being mutable is great because it affords you so much choice. But unlike those fixed or cardinal energies, who have a home base, flexible Gemini can spin around in the air so much that she can lose her bearings. Who are you? Are you the easygoing, fun-loving companion, the sassy, sexy conversationalist, the compassionate, soothing, intuitive friend? You're all that, but when you're tired or stressed you won't know which "you" fits.

That mutability makes you a fantastic date. You can pick up on a guy's mood and complement it. Just don't lose yourself in figuring him out, or you won't know who you are anymore. It's easy for you to go along for the ride, harder to stop in the moment and know what you're feeling. Sometimes you don't know if you even like him until after you've agreed to go out again. You're such a good little socializer that you forget that you can say no and that you don't have to like everyone (but it's so easy!).

When you get scared or anxious, you can get a little sharp. Watch the bite and bravado in your words. There's no reason to be defensive—just get some sleep or take a break. Gemini AstroBabes don't like to miss the action, but it's better than having nervous exhaustion. And when you're running on empty, you might lose track of what you're saying, or how much you've said, and that's not the best way to exert those flirtatious powers of romance.

Know your mind, watch your mouth, and take

a breath every now and then. It's easier to make meaningful eye contact when you're quiet.

AstroBabe Planetary Pulse: 2
Gemini Guy Planetary Pulse: 1
Compatible Signs: Gemini, Sagittarius, Libra
Magnetic Sign: Scorpio

Sun in Cancer

ELEMENT: WATER
ENERGY: CARDINAL

It's hard to grasp the concept of the Sun placed in the sign most connected to the Moon. Which planet has more influence? The Sun and its outgoing energy, or the Moon and its internal mystery?

The Sun in Cancer takes on some qualities of the Moon. Energy will shift from hot to cold, earning Cancers the label of "moody." The Sun is still vibrant and bright, but instead of pushing out, its energy is more embracing, grasping, and complacent. Cancers are domestic, nurturing, mothering. They create a space where they can be vibrant on their own terms.

AstroBabes in the sign of Cancer are the loving, hand-holding, soothing girlfriends and wives. If your Sun is in Cancer, the right guys gravitate to you because they know that you are ultrafeminine, caring, and loyal.

Cancer is a water sign (emotional) and a cardinal sign (directed), so AstroBabes in Cancer are very good at being loving. You were born knowing how to love and nurture, and if you want to express your love through having children, you'll find that motherhood comes naturally. Cancer is the Crab, as you know, and that Crab has a hard outer shell, tough to penetrate. Inside, it's all mush, just sweet, tender mush. To earn a place in your tender heart, a guy is going to have to prove his worth. You don't let just anyone in. You might have friends who flirt and date for sport, but that's not you. It doesn't amuse you in the least.

You like to love and to be loved. You would never walk away from someone you love without long and deep consideration. While you Cancer girls are practically irresistible to a guy who wants a traditional relationship, you have to be careful of the dark side of your sign. It's called "S'Mothering."

Let's say you're in a relationship and your guy is going through a rough time. You take special care to help him through it. That's just fine. But when you kind of like the feeling of being the caretaker, you can start creating more opportunities to do it. Then you're mothering him. If you keep it up too long, you'll be smothering him. "S'Mothering" is a trait of Cancer AstroBabes that you don't necessarily want to exercise. S'Mothering is a passion killer, and even though you're into domesticity, you still want to enjoy passion, sensuality, and sexual play. (That's how you make babies, right?)

Be on alert if you feel more comfortable making dinner than making love. You need both in a good relationship.

AstroBabe Planetary Pulse: 3
Cancer Guy Planetary Pulse: 2
Compatible Signs: Taurus, Virgo, Scorpio
Magnetic Sign: Libra

Sun in Leo

ELEMENT: FIRE
ENERGY: FIXED

As the Moon excels in Cancer, so does the Sun shine in Leo. This is the Sun's sign, its vibrant, glowing life force. Sun in Leo is a happy energy: positive, optimistic, willing to make a go of anything. Leo is the leader, the king of the zodiac. You don't mind if your loyal subjects cast admiring gazes in your direction—in fact, you love it!

AstroBabes with Sun in Leo really enjoy the pursuit of love. Sure, you can handle a long-term relationship, but dating is fun and there's no need to rush things. You like the sport of flirting. You love to be appreciated. You have such a physical presence that it's hard for you *not* to stand out.

Your inner joy is attractive to many people and you are very generous. This combination can cause you to be overwhelmed by quantity and feel a lack in quality when it comes to suitors. Guys who have courage and are at ease with your glow are your favorites. You don't take kindly to wusses. Develop your strategies for discerning from the masses those guys who are willing and able to take you out in proper style.

It's not that you're a snob, but you have standards. Your girlfriends might find you kind of picky, especially if you consider the number of guys who want to go out with you. There might be some jealousy in the wings, but you don't take any notice. Most Leos are accustomed to it.

So what exactly is the dark side of one with such a sunny nature? The dark side of self-esteem is that *too* much is not a good thing. If you have your Leo pride, your Leo leadership, and your Leo fixed energy all fired up at once, you might wind up alone. Leos can get a tad self-involved and forget that other people need their chance to shine, too. The dark side of Leo typically appears in childhood and again in dating. You won't have a clue why he didn't call back, because hey, you had a great time. But when you think about it, did he get a word in edgewise?

Leos are highly knowledgeable people. They like

to share their worldly advice. They like to motivate others. From a less flattering angle, they look like lecturers. And nobody likes to go out with a lecturer—it's just not fun.

There's no keeping you down, though. Even if you don't get your way all the time, even if romance fizzles, you recover quickly and resume your shiny, happy self. You are always up for a good time. Friends and family are just as important as finding the right guy. You take your time in romance because you want to get it just right.

AstroBabes with Sun in Leo are happy, healthy, and great at flirting. Go out and have some fun, date, and fall in love. It comes so naturally that you won't even break a sweat.

AstroBabe Planetary Pulse: 4
Leo Guy Planetary Pulse: 4
Compatible Signs: Gemini, Sagittarius, Aries
Magnetic Sign: Pisces

Sun in Virgo

ELEMENT: EARTH

ENERGY: MUTABLE

When your Sun shines in Virgo, it lights up the gentle, loving, helping nature of your character. Virgo AstroBabes are always good-looking; they are particular about appearance and have excellent taste, of course. Virgo is the sign of the Virgin, but that's not about your romantic life. The Virgin holds the bundle of harvest wheat, emerging from the long summer to reap the abundance of the autumn. She provides what we need to get us through the winter. And so AstroBabes with the Sun in Virgo also provide, taking care of relationships in their own way.

You're more thoughtful than other Sun signs and some might think you're more serious. That may be true, but you do also have an excellent sense of humor, which is mighty useful for flirting. You don't like coarse humor, but there are occasions where you can be innocently raunchy—it's a great crowd-pleaser.

You can verbally joust as well as tease, but don't

let it go too far. You have to be able to take what you can dish out, and—admit it—you're a bit sensitive. When you're feeling good about yourself you can push the limits, but when you turn your demand for perfection inward, you can get tough on yourself. And if you feel less than perfect, you can feel terribly vulnerable to others. Sometimes you're a little insecure; don't judge it—just let it rest. Sooner or later the world reminds you how wonderful you are.

In romance, you like a good, smart counterpart—someone who is active, interesting, and able to understand your complexities. You have a lot of rules, so it's best to find someone who either has similar standards or doesn't mind yours. You won't enjoy a relationship that's a power struggle; it's not productive and you'll get bored. Often, you'll meet a guy, date him once or twice, decide he's not for you, and make him a lifelong friend. You're great at transitioning guys without hurting their feelings.

The darker side of Virgo AstroBabes lies in the need to take care of others. You are a sucker for wounded puppies. I'm not talking pets here—taking in real animals is fine—but the guys who catch your attention! The ones who are angry, lonely, even addicted; you name it—you like it. You put out a lot of energy to help others—that's just what you do. But in a relationship, it's not easy to maintain the balance between love and caretaking. If you find yourself always being the one doing the caring, you're in the wrong place. It is your spiritual task to learn to let others help you, to allow yourself to rest and let go of being the one in charge.

Once you find a guy who likes to nurture, you're in for the long haul. You'll enjoy both giving and receiving, and that's what you're all about.

AstroBabe Planetary Pulse: 2
Virgo Guy Planetary Pulse: 3
Compatible Signs: Taurus, Cancer, Scorpio
Magnetic Sign: Aquarius

Sun in Libra

ELEMENT: AIR
ENERGY: CARDINAL

AstroBabes with the Sun in Libra are not exactly novices when it comes to romance. Libra is the sign that rules partnership—as well as balance, justice, and peace. Born under Libra, your life is almost an arrow seeking the perfect bull's-eye in the area of romance. Ruled by Venus, the sign of Libra loves love, harmony, beauty, and all that is pleasurable. As an air sign, Libra seeks knowledge; to know the whole story is to be in harmony.

Libra AstroBabes move through life careful not to cause disruption, and are eager to restore harmony when things are not going smoothly. Libras love good and interesting ideas, but tolerate people who aren't as intellectual, too. Libras are discerning but not snobs, and are curious but not nosy. AstroBabes born under Libra are good flirts but never take it too far, and are born girlfriends because they love to be in partnership.

It's rare to find a Libra woman who is not in some kind of relationship, but if you are without a guy, you're learning one of those important spiritual lessons: to be alone. In your opposite sign, Aries, the task is to learn to maintain freedom while being in a relationship. In Libra, it's to learn that being alone helps a relationship become stronger.

The mistake most often made by Libra Astro-

Babes is to be in a relationship just for the sake of being in a relationship. You're the girl who always has a boyfriend. It may seem better than being solo, but you don't give yourself much of a chance to find out how much fun it is to play the field. You have to learn how to be on your own at some point (and not to panic when you are). Once you do, you'll be able to find an even better guy. You can take time to interview the candidates—there'll be plenty of them!

In constantly seeking balance, Libra is notoriously bad at making up her mind. If you're ever in the position of "torn between two lovers," you'll be completely against the wall. When you're with one, he's *it*. When you're with the other, you don't want to hurt him. Libra AstroBabes have been known to create romantic chaos and, on occasion, break up and get back together about a million times. It's hard being an air sign, because you're not grounded. You can't access your practicality as easily as the other Venus-ruled sign, Taurus. You just shift this way and that, trying to find the right balance in an impossible situation.

Taking the time to find out who you are on your own will help you figure out any romantic situation.

You have to take yourself out of the game if you want to get perspective. When romance is healthy, you won't question it. And it will be so easy, you won't have to make any effort to find your equilibrium.

So don't rush things. You'll find the right guy when you take time out and date yourself once in a while.

AstroBabe Planetary Pulse: 4
Libra Guy Planetary Pulse: 5
Compatible Signs: Libra, Leo, Sagittarius
Magnetic Sign: Cancer

Sun in Scorpio

ELEMENT: WATER
ENERGY: FIXED

You've more than likely heard about Scorpio's secrecy, passion, intensity, and privacy. The sign is famous for it. AstroBabes with Sun in Scorpio are born for lovemaking—it's the sign that rules sex, as well as death and change. It's not what you'd call a light sign, but when you learn to harness that amazing power, you can do anything.

Scorpio is the sign that never follows orders. No one can tell you what to do. That's part of being a fixed sign as well as being so intelligent. You have your own plans, your own sensibility about when it's the right time to move. You are very deep and creative, and you have an amazing dark side. Remember, in darkness there is wonderful mystery and imagination. You're born with a direct line to the universe, a high-speed connection to creative resources of every kind. It's your talent and your right, but it takes time to get used to the power of this great gift. Being a powerful Scorpio takes a lot of practice, patience, and experimentation.

As an AstroBabe with Sun in Scorpio, when you're hot to trot there's no denying your charisma, but when you're not, forget it. There's no middle ground for you. In fact, you've earned the nickname "hot ice." When you're feeling comfortable with yourself and keeping a positive attitude, there's no one sexier. Forget words; all you need to do is walk into a room and guys fall into line. You're warm, charming, friendly ... and very misleading. People will take to you and think you're so easygoing, then be totally freaked-out when they accidentally probe your sensitive side and you lash out. Scorpio Astro-Babes have rule books (secret rules, never to be revealed!), and if someone happens to break a rule or even bend it by accident, it's over. It takes a long time for Scorpios to forgive, and frankly, they never forget.

Your feelings about romance are intense. Love means passion; flirtation is just not interesting. Scorpio AstroBabes like to dive into the deep waters of love and all that it comes with, but the guy has to be just right: passionate, deep, and tolerant. He's got to be patient and sensitive and smart. You both have a lot of energy and want to use it. Travel, water sports, making love—it's all good.

Intimacy is incredible when you find it, but to get there you have to journey through the land of vulnerability, possibly your least favorite place—for Scorpios like to be in control of everything, and being vulnerable, accessible, means not being in control. Scorpio AstroBabes are great actresses—check out Julia Roberts, Meg Ryan, Jodie Foster—you know you have that in you, too. But that means you can act as if you're open but still hold back. And that short-circuits the whole idea of intimacy.

Once you let your guard down and find someone with whom you can build trust, you'll find true love and passion. Maintain the ability to be open and intimate, and you'll find long-term love.

AstroBabe Planetary Pulse: 4
Scorpio Guy Planetary Pulse: 4
Compatible Signs: Taurus, Pisces, Capricorn
Magnetic Sign: Gemini

Sun in Sagittarius

ELEMENT: FIRE
ENERGY: MUTABLE

Happy-go-lucky Sagittarius, you let the Sun shine into your world through adventure, risk taking, and travel. You're a restless spirit filled with curiosity, the desire to know more of the world. Fearless and resilient, you do make a good traveler. You can go anywhere and feel at home. But can you *stay* at home? That's another story.

AstroBabes with Sun in Sagittarius are easy and breezy. You love a challenge and you love your independence. You won't say no to love, but at the same time, it can get in the way of your plans. You have stacks of energy, so that's not the problem; it's just that you have so much that you want to do, to see, to experience. Any guy who hangs with you has to be game. He has to be comfortable with risks, because you like them. And he has to have his own interests and goals, because you don't want him tagging along with yours.

It takes a careful combination of zest and dedication to maintain a relationship when you're a Sagittarian AstroBabe. You absolutely need a challenge—an easy guy is not a fun guy. But you also have to find a guy who understands you, and that takes time, focus, and interest. It's big-game fishing for you—the harder, the better, and even if you make a great catch, you might think there's another challenge out there for you. You're the girl who doesn't settle down.

Sagittarian AstroBabes are smart and honest, sometimes too much so. "Frank to a fault" and "painfully direct" are the terms most often used to describe you when you share an opinion. Whatever—you don't really care. You cannot bear lies and you don't intend to propagate them. If a guy can't take it, he's out.

The darker side of Sagittarius is restlessness. You're not a cozy, stay-at-home character. You need to *move!* Even if you're confined to quarters, you need to read, surf the Internet, talk on the phone. You're probably addicted to your cell phone or BlackBerry. You simply cannot be tied down, and if you feel as if you are, you wriggle free in one way or another.

This is fatal to relationships that require you to yield to someone else's choices or power. Those won't work. You need freedom to pursue your goals, even if those goals are raising kids and being a good partner. You have to do it your own way. Forget having a master; you'd rather be single than subordinate.

Romance is only one item on your long list of areas to explore. It's easy to get distracted or push it to the bottom of your list. But pay attention to the realm of love and you'll find there's plenty of adventure in it to keep you busy until your next safari.

AstroBabe Planetary Pulse: 3
Sagittarius Guy Planetary Pulse: 3
Compatible Signs: Libra, Gemini, Leo
Magnetic Sign: Pisces

Sun in Capricorn

ELEMENT: EARTH
ENERGY: CARDINAL

The character of Capricorn is often misunderstood and misinterpreted in magazine horoscopes. Because Capricorn is the sign of careers, authority, hard work, and perseverance, its planetary movements are all too often reduced to achievements or setbacks; serious stuff instead of lighthearted engagements. The reality is different. Sure, Capricorn is a focused, directed sign (that cardinal energy) and it does have clear goals. But fun and love can be goals, too, and when they are, there's no sign that enjoys itself more than Capricorn.

AstroBabes born under the sign of Capricorn carry a natural dignity and poise. You walk in high heels without tripping. Your hair never has a bad day. Typically, you're self-assured and glide toward what you want with the clear intention of achieving it. This is what confounds others—the fact that you can focus so calmly, without showing any signs of stress. It can seem like you don't have the same feelings that more emotionally communicative people have. You do, of course. You're a worrier, but you don't show it. Even if you make a speech with spinach in your teeth, you won't let anyone see you freak out about it. You feel safer if no one knows you're embarrassed. You don't move beyond your own comfort level.

You are often the late bloomer in the zodiac, but you do, indeed, bloom. Capricorn is characterized as slow to start but fast to finish; this pretty well describes your careful approach in life and the fact that once your goal is in sight, you move swiftly toward achievement.

In matters of love, this works well. You don't date a large quantity of guys. You don't need to flirt and try out all different kinds. You won't love often, but you will love well. You're a quality—not quantity—type. It may take longer for you to find that one true love, but when you do, it's well worth it. You won't settle for someone who isn't right; you'd rather be on your own.

The darker side of Capricorn is probably what makes those monthly horoscopes so obsessed with your serious side. It's true that when you're under the gun, you hunker down and work hard. It's also true that you can face disappointment with dignity, that problems and obstacles don't deter you from what you want to achieve. And yes, you can be aloof and dispassionate, to the point of being cold. This is all because you simply don't want to show your vulnerable interior. And this is what makes it harder for guys to get to know you and why you take your time revealing your true, tender self. You have to be comfortable with the circumstance, and once you are, you can let your guard down, slowly.

Not everyone is going to want to stick around and wait for you to feel comfortable. I know, you don't care—they're not worth it. But this slow-to-warm behavior is what gives you the reputation for being less emotional and more pragmatic.

Ultimately, you'll learn that having a bad hair day or making a mistake in front of someone else isn't going to kill you. It's only going to make you more lovable. So open up to love (and your own vulnerability) and enjoy it just as much as, if not more than, every other sign in the zodiac.

AstroBabe Planetary Pulse: 2
Capricorn Guy Planetary Pulse: 4
Compatible Signs: Scorpio, Pisces, Cancer
Magnetic Sign: Gemini

Sun in Aquarius

ELEMENT: AIR
ENERGY: FIXED
When the Sun shines in the Water Bearer's sign of Aquarius, the world is illuminated. As an air sign, Aquarians are typically thoughtful and considerate, and enjoy conversation. They are also inventive, eccentric, unconfined, perceptive, and unpredictable! Even though the sign rules friendship, an Aquarian does not tend to have many intimate friends;

she's just too into her own thing to give time to others.

In romance, you AstroBabes with an Aquarian Sun are the rebels. It isn't easy to predict who will turn your head, from banker to ballet dancer. Minds are sexy, ideas are alluring, and a guy who sambas to the beat of his own drum is fascinating. You can't stand someone telling you what to do or what to think. Any guy who wants to be with you has to give you your space.

Because Aquarius is a fixed sign, you can be impossibly stubborn. The darker side of Aquarius is what comes of the combination of your independent thinking with your fixed energy. AstroBabes with Sun in Aquarius cannot stand to live what feels like a life of conformity, but seeking out the avant-garde for the sake of variety can lead to trouble. A guy might seem like a sexy, charismatic rebel but turn out to be simply angry, unrealized potential. Once your interest wanes, your patience will, too.

Aquarius AstroBabes love to flirt with someone who has something to say. Small talk isn't fun. You'd prefer to be hanging out with your friends rather than trying to make conversation with a bore. Art, theater, music, and most other creative fields will lead you to people who interest you even if you don't pursue a career in those areas.

You're also a tolerant, patient girlfriend. Once you do fall in love, you will find that you are inspired and stimulated by having a partner. Real love doesn't make you feel as if you're trapped in an elevator with bad music. It makes you want to compose your own melodies, design your own house, and, of course, hop to the beat of your two drums. You'll enjoy doing things together as well as the freedom to do something on your own.

Spontaneity will always be your romantic spice of choice, so don't let go of your impulses. Investigating new places or events, following hunches, and simply being able to thrill to new ideas will refresh your relationship. Avoid too much routine, or you'll find yourself on that dreaded elevator, going down, down, down.

AstroBabe Planetary Pulse: 1
Aquarian Guy Planetary Pulse: 1
Compatible Signs: Sagittarius, Aries, Gemini
Magnetic Sign: Leo

Sun in Pisces

ELEMENT: WATER
ENERGY: MUTABLE

The Sun in Pisces is a light on infinite creativity, dreams, and the concept of bliss. Neptune rules this water sign, and there he sits on the bottom of the sea, trident in hand, enjoying untold beauty and holding the power of life itself. From this dark, mysterious place, Pisces inherits a longing for love on unconditional terms, for an ocean of warm, supportive waters that feed the need for comfort.

You AstroBabes with the Sun in Pisces are capable of endless love, compassion, and connection. In a greater sense, you love the world, supporting (in your heart) utopian notions of world peace, true goodwill, and abundance all around. In romantic love, you believe in "happily ever after" and hope, at some point in your life, to experience it. You're apt to tell the story of your life beginning with "Once upon a time," but your love life will be less dramatic than fairy tales—with no fatalities.

Pisces AstroBabes are the most romantic sign of

the zodiac. You can fantasize yourself into complete happiness and then, upon waking, commit yourself to making your dreams come true.

Here's the struggle for Pisces. You don't care all that much for reality—it doesn't measure up. Your utopian longings allow you to believe that true love and true happiness do exist. And that you'll find them if only you keep searching. In one way, that's true. You can meet a guy who is your true romantic hero. In another way, it's complete fantasy, because that guy will be no more capable of sustaining the heights of romantic oblivion than you are. It's impossible. The disappointments you come to know as a romantic youth become the realities (not such bad realities) of adulthood. You are more than ready and able to live a life that is happier than anything most others ever dream of, but you have to accustom yourself to the fact that you won't be living on cloud nine every day.

Disappointment, and by that I mean reality, can lead you to one of two reactions. The first (and preferable) route is to let go of your standards, feel tolerance rather than revulsion for less-than-perfect situations, and ease into making the best of your love and your life. The second route, taken at least once in a Pisces AstroBabe's lifetime, is the "tune out and turn off" option. Your sign is the Fish, as you almost certainly know, and you are the original "cold fish."

That said, give imperfect love a chance. Pisces AstroBabes are a gift to the world. When you're feeling hopeful, secure, and alert, there is no one who is more loving, forgiving, nurturing, and sensual. You are a joy to be around and a source of great pleasure to all of us, even if we're not your husband.

AstroBabe Planetary Pulse: 5
Pisces Guy Planetary Pulse: 3
Compatible Signs: Taurus, Capricorn, Scorpio
Magnetic Sign: Sagittarius

THREE

The Moon

AstroBabes, it's all about the Moon. Like you, the Moon is a reflective, mysterious, changing feminine being.

The Moon is our best friend, ladies. We live through our emotions, our fertility, our intuition. That's what the Moon rules. We like to shift—to feel open and full and then to retreat, to be alone. If you watch the moon, you'll see how much it influences your life as it moves through its cycle, waxing (growing to full) and waning (shrinking to the new moon).

The Moon stands for domesticity, for maternal

instincts. The ancients used to look at the full moon and see the pregnant moon goddess. I see the full moon and step carefully into the world. Ever hear the origin of the word "lunacy"? You got it—"luna" is the moon, and the full moon notably increases strange moods and events. We don't see pregnant moon goddesses, but we might see other weird happenings.

The Moon isn't just for women, of course, and you will learn a lot about a guy just by knowing what his Moon is, too. But for us women, the Moon is a really strong ingredient in our romantic abilities.

Take, for instance, a fire sign Moon. You know that the qualities associated with fire signs are fearlessness, passion, adventure, outgoing energy. If your Moon is in a fire sign, you'll be resilient in love. You'll say, "Can do, let's go," or, "No, thanks." No shrinking violets here. Now assume that you have the Moon in a water element. Water signs are more internal, deep feeling, and careful, so you won't want to go adventuring in the world of relationships. Similarly, earth sign Moons are a little more practical and cautious, while air sign Moons tend to float about more, considering and sampling a variety of romantic opportunities.

Next, combine a Sun sign with a Moon sign and you start to see the complexity of your romantic nature. If you combine an outgoing fire sign Sun with a cautious and shy water Moon sign, what do you get? Answer: an outgoing woman who is careful about her romantic life. Reverse the combination for a water sign Sun and a fire sign Moon. You'll have a quiet nature but an adventurous romantic life.

These, of course, are broad strokes outlining what is a more complex reality. The point is, you may find that your Moon sign is very different from your Sun sign, and you need to pay attention to those differences. Of all the planets we cover in *AstroBabe*, the Moon is the most important.

It is your subtle guide in every aspect of life: your intuition, the whisper of attraction, the impulse of passion, and the dedication of loyalty. The moon is your conscience and your secret life. Explore all it offers you and know more about yourself than you have ever known before.

AstroBabe Moon Secret

If your Moon or Venus is the same as his Moon or Venus, you'll have a strong emotional bond.

Moon in Aries

The exuberance and energy of Aries fuels the Moon's influence in your life. You have an excellent imagination and a positive attitude about life and romance. You are not going to shrink in the face of romantic opportunity, but you won't forgo your independence for just anyone.

Aries Moons are fiery, and they thrive on a diet of passion and edginess. Forget the "same old thing." You won't care for the slow and steady type unless your Sun overrules your Moon. In some way, either in romance or in the passion of your work, you need to be challenged and kept on your toes.

In some cases, the Aries Moon prefers independence to the contractual state of marriage. Astro-Babes with strong Aries influences will inevitably find a unique balance between the softness of love and the spice of life, between giving and receiving on an emotional level. You don't need to be looked after or coddled; in fact, you would dislike being thought of as weak or fragile.

You also have a little temper problem, girls. I say this because I have an Aries Moon and I know first-hand about being a hothead. Passions run hot, sometimes too hot, and you might just explode out of the top of your head if you don't find a place to let off some steam. AstroBabes with Moon in Aries like to get physical. The gym or the outdoors is a great place to shake it off.

An important aspect of having the Moon in Aries is being the adventurer, the conqueror. In the pursuit of romance, you like a good chase. It can't be too easy or you won't think it's worth it. In that respect, if your interest isn't being held by your current guy, that hot little head of yours might turn.

Impulsive? Oh yeah, that's you. As you get older you won't flip this little switch as often. But if you're a young AstroBabe, know that you have that zodiacal DNA that can shift at any given moment. I wouldn't call you "fickle" so much as "hard to pin down." You're a butterfly, and they don't like pins!

AstroBabe Planetary Pulse: 2
Aries Moon Guy Planetary Pulse: 3

Moon in Taurus

All the lovely qualities of Taurus reflected by the light of the Moon mean a loving, calm emotional flow. You have solid, steady intuition and pretty good judgment. People find you easy to be with, easy to like, because you can be counted on.

AstroBabes with a Taurus Moon don't tend to feel anxious or worried about love. It comes to you because you're pretty approachable, you're undemanding, and you can be very sensual. You can sort through those guys who are interested and willing but not totally right for you, and can skip over the inconsistent or fly-by-night types. You have a steady heart and you need a steady guy.

What you love in a guy is a lot like what you have to offer him back: loyalty, steadiness, security.

A guy who says one thing and does another is possibly the worst match for you. And you'll show him the door after one strike, not three. You're nobody's fool when it comes to fakes.

On the other hand, you can be gradually misled into a bad relationship if it happens slowly, and especially if it started out perfectly: the old "bait and switch." This sometimes happens when a guy makes a fabulous boyfriend for six months to a year and then suddenly reveals that he's really a bum. Some girls get it right away and off he goes. But if you have a Taurus Moon, you're going to stick it out, waiting for that great guy to resurface. Sometimes he does! Sadly, most often he's long gone and in his place is someone you would not have fallen for in the first place. Here's where the Taurus Moon hits a bump. Loyal to a fault. There is going to be a time when you have to admit that he's not right, he's not the one, and you have to move on. It takes time. You can't be rushed into this. Often your friends will have given up before you get to this point.

The upside to waiting too long to get out of a relationship is that you're completely over it by the time you leave. So you're ready for a new one pretty quickly. Take heart—AstroBabes with Moon in Taurus don't have a tough time meeting guys. Use that as an incentive to get out of a relationship that doesn't work anymore.

AstroBabe Planetary Pulse: 4

Taurus Moon Guy Planetary Pulse: 4

Moon in Gemini

The Moon's internal, intuitive, mysterious energy finds the sign of Gemini a little confusing. The Moon likes to feel. Gemini likes to talk. The Moon likes to quietly come and go; Gemini likes to dart around finding new entertainment. The Moon is the mother, and the sign of Gemini is the child who can't sit still. So what happens when the Moon is placed in this airy, mutable sign?

You AstroBabes with Moon in Gemini are very bright, very friendly, and prone to storytelling. The Moon is exceptionally creative in Gemini, and emotions, feelings, hunches, and premonitions come spilling out, unedited, and sometimes without fact-checking.

Gemini Moons are flirtatious, fun, and friendly. This planetary sign is an excellent combination for meeting guys and getting to know them. Your guy's got to be interesting and he's got to be able to keep up with you—no small feat. You like to mix it up. If he likes to be quiet and go deep, you have a challenge on your hands. You won't be amused by anyone who isn't easy to talk to. You won't be entertained by pulling information out of him like a dentist pulling a tooth. And can you sit still for him?

Gemini Moons are very creative, even ingenious. You need a guy who is smart. Remember that thing about storytelling? AstroBabes with Gemini Moons do spin a good yarn. You can tell a true story and embellish it (purely for amusement) and all of a sudden, your little tale has become a great, dramatic saga.

Your challenge is to find quiet. Keep your tongue from wagging and let him get a word in. That way you'll actually get to know him and not just amuse him. Guys like to talk, too.

Remember, Gemini is the sign of the Twins.

AstroBabes with this Moon can be inclined to have two relationships at once. It goes without saying that you can date more than one guy at a time, but you can be something of a two-timer, too. When you can't keep track of who's who and you can't remember what you said to which one, that's when it's time to dial it down and take a good rest.

The world might see you as a little dizzy, but we know the truth: you're just fascinating. When you find a guy who keeps you focused, you know you've hit gold.

AstroBabe Planetary Pulse: 3
Gemini Moon Guy Planetary Pulse: 2

Moon in Cancer

Girl, you *are* the Moon. Cancer is the most powerful place for the Moon to express its mystery, love, and emotional expanse. AstroBabes with the Moon in Cancer are deeply caring, very creative, and capable of enduring love.

Your emotional self flows easily through life, feeling, shifting, taking in and reflecting back what others feel. You can turn it off, of course, since Cancer's Crab has a hard outer shell that keeps you from being overwhelmed by feeling. But you need to keep yourself open because your intuition, which is irrevocably tied to your emotions, is your single most important source of truth and information. You can't shut down completely, or you lose that internal compass.

You can't help the fact that you're deep. And why should you? You can soothe, smooth, and shush anyone's cares away. You make those you love feel safe, warm, and secure. Now, what's the matter with that? Dating. That's the problem.

When it comes to love, deep love, you're the best. But put you in a situation where you have to be light, bright, and carefree, and you almost have to fake it. It's not like you don't know how to have fun; it's just that you like to carefully pick your playmates. It's hard to let go and be silly with a bunch of strangers. You're not grabbing the mike for your turn at the karaoke bar because all those people staring at you would be too gruesome.

Let's not get too down, though. You are the best date when the right guy comes along. This guy likes your knowing eyes, your steady energy. He's intrigued by your ability to hold back and to be discerning. He likes your depth, although he'll only sense it at first. Once you let him inside that emotional shell, he'll never want to leave. You're the coziest, deepest, most accepting heart he'll ever want to know.

Ultimately, you'll prefer a long-term relationship to a fun date. You're born to nurture, to mother, to embrace. Let's just say it: AstroBabes with Moon in Cancer like to get married. There's no problem with that, either, but you usually have to date a little before you get there.

Don't be afraid to take a few turns at love. There's a ton of it just waiting for you.

AstroBabe Planetary Pulse: 2
Cancer Moon Guy Planetary Pulse: 2

Moon in Leo

AstroBabes with the Moon in Leo are the lion-hearted females of the zodiac. Brave, purposeful, magnetic, and proud, you have a heart of solid gold.

The Moon in Leo is ardent. You are committed to your beliefs and you don't mind sharing them with others. You're also funny, and an excellent sense of humor is very important to you in romance. You love to be in love; you love to love. You have a great time with kids and you know how to be a kid at any age in your life.

Your natural exuberance is very attractive to guys. Your Moon has an inner radiance and you can turn it up so much that the entire room will notice you. You don't mind being popular; it comes naturally and you handle it with ease. You don't like to make people feel uncomfortable, so you don't let anyone walk away feeling dejected. They might be rejected, but they'll still smile.

Your fixed nature is also very advantageous when you put it to good use. You could, by preferring to leave well enough alone, stay too long with someone who is no longer a great mate. At some point, you'll come to your senses, though, and then you won't waste a minute and move on.

There's not much that irritates you, but someone else's pity is one thing that does. You don't like to be the center of attention when the news is bad or your situation is difficult. That's enough to spur you on to charge ahead and make things better. Lemonade from lemons is your special recipe.

Here's what you need to look out for on the darker side. You do like attention, and you can mistake someone's flattering interest for genuine caring. You're so eager to take in the stroking that you're not too concerned about ulterior motives. After you're fooled once or twice, however, it shouldn't happen again.

Second, because the Leo heart loves to give love, you might overlook the importance of receiving. Open your own heart up to being touched by another's love. Being on the receiving end requires a certain amount of vulnerability. You don't always like that.

Leo Moons like to lead, not submit. Consider that revealing a little fragility or vulnerability is a simple act of love.

AstroBabe Planetary Pulse: 4
Leo Moon Guy Planetary Pulse: 5

Moon in Virgo

The mysterious Moon in Virgo lends AstroBabes a strong intuitive sense, a clever mind, and an unassuming way of making dreams come true. Emotions and imagination settle into organization, knowledge, and a sensitivity to environments, both physical and emotional.

Virgo doesn't like to make a spectacle of itself, and when your Moon glows in this sign, it gives you a low-key, adjustable, and purposeful energy. Being mutable, Virgo makes the Moon emotionally flexible. This helps in keeping you calibrated to your environment, but when vibes get complicated, you can suffer from anxiety. AstroBabes with Virgo Moons can be the most verbally amusing partygoers and then suddenly, if the stakes get too high, snap into high-strung harpies. It's hard to be as sensitive as you are, because you pick up a lot of nonverbal communication. While someone else might be asking, "How's it going?" you could be feeling, "What the hell is going on?" You're sensitive—you can't help it.

For that reason, you tend to be a bit critical of others—it's born of protecting yourself. You can't tolerate harsh tones, loud voices, boisterous stupidity. You don't care for crudeness, noise, or dirt. It's just not your thing—no fraternity keggers for you! You're also particular about food and drink. What others might not understand is that you have to be—your body is very sensitive, too.

Where does this leave you? Stay with your intuition; it will lead you to the right romance, the right place, the right atmosphere. Don't be persuaded to do anything you don't want to do. If it feels wrong, don't go. The people and events that will attract you are going to be genuinely good for you. You don't have to be uncomfortable just to meet people or have a good time. Don't forget, there are guys just like you, too. They'll also be finding fun in places that aren't loud and crowded.

Honor your inner self. You have a lot of love in you to give to the right person. Take your time to find him.

AstroBabe Planetary Pulse: 3
Virgo Moon Guy Planetary Pulse: 2

Moon in Libra

Balance-seeking Libra takes the emotional Moon into realms of harmony, beauty, and peace. You Astro-Babes with the Moon in Libra are intuitive, charming, thoughtful, and careful. However, the moon's natural phases are not easy for the sign of Libra, and equilibrium must constantly be negotiated; it's never permanent.

In that sense, AstroBabes with the Moon in Libra are always making the best of situations and do their best to avoid conflict. Being an easygoing, naturally engaging flirt is your norm. You have no problem finding something to say, and you are, of course, very clever. The Libra Moon is also fashion savvy, so you're pretty well put together. You can be a guy magnet.

It's when things get complicated that you lose your balance. Anger is not a comfortable feeling. Other people's anger is even worse. You can sense someone else's irritation, especially if it is directed at you, and even if outwardly you pretend not to notice, inside you're freaking out. Getting used to dealing with conflict is a lifelong mission, and it won't go away. You've tried the head-in-the-sand technique? It doesn't work. The other cowardly option is to freeze out the other person, turning cold and aloof instead of staying open and vulnerable. You'll learn, if you haven't already, that an ice princess isn't a great date.

Being clever, the Libra Moon can consider and evaluate any situation. You can basically figure out how to get any guy. But what do you do with him once you get him?

If you find out you don't like him a whole lot, or at least not "in that way," don't try to convince yourself to stay with him simply to avoid conflict. Melt the ice and be honest with the poor guy; that way you'll regain your equilibrium more quickly. If you find that you're talking yourself into him by saying, "I think I feel . . . ," you're already in trouble. Thinking too much alienates you from your emotions. When you don't know what you feel, you can't make a great romantic connection.

In the end, AstroBabes with Libra Moons are great romantics. The lessons you learn in allowing yourself to feel, not think, through life will only make you happier.

AstroBabe Planetary Pulse: 5
Libra Moon Guy Planetary Pulse: 4

Moon in Scorpio

As the Moon shifts into the sign of Scorpio, it defines perhaps the most complex emotional character in the zodiac. The moon has phases, and Scorpio, the sign of sex, death, and change, is intensely defined by highs and lows, light and darkness. This makes for an AstroBabe with very strong emotions that are controlled and seldom permitted to surface.

AstroBabes with Moon in Scorpio are very independent and extremely capable. You can do just about whatever you set your mind and heart to. Because you can be very shy, professional challenges are sometimes preferable to exploring the social or emotional parts of life. Of course, you're an amazing friend and you'll always have a loyal handful of those you hold close. But intimacy and love—these you tend to avoid.

The Moon in Scorpio is the enigmatic woman in a film noir, the spy, the beauty with a hidden past. You exude mystery—often because it really exists. AstroBabes with Moon in Scorpio feel as if they have a "past," whether or not anyone else would consider that to be true. This feeling can make you act more reserved and create more mystery around you, and that means guys are intrigued, provoked into wanting to know more. You will either run away or very slowly reveal yourself to someone who interests you, too. But no one will ever think you wear your heart on your sleeve. You're inclined to be suspicious of any guy who comes on to you (and you have impeccable radar for that), so you tend to keep your guard up for a long time. Beware of paranoia, though. You can limit yourself if you get too protective.

Ultimately, you choose your mate carefully and progress to intimacy when you're ready. How far you go is up to you. You can go deeply and fulfill your desire for intense connection, or you can keep things manageably close. Allow him to show you his comfort level and you'll find it's easy to go the deeper route.

AstroBabe Planetary Pulse: 1
Scorpio Moon Guy Planetary Pulse: 1

Moon in Sagittarius

The mysterious, changing Moon finds it hard to relax in the adventure-loving, fiery sign of Sagittarius. The Moon's depths don't have time to settle before there's something else to feel, to emote, to intuit. However, the light side of the Moon is very comfortable as it basks in the energy of Sagittarius' escapades.

An AstroBabe with Moon in Sagittarius is not easy to pin down. Some might call you fickle; some might say you're a love-'em-and-leave-'em type. You won't be around to hear it, though, because once things get dull, you get lost. You are independent, boss-avoiding, and not all that interested in popular opinion. This is ideal for bold, joyful relationships as long as they last. You have an uncanny ability to find guys who are diamonds in the rough, polish them into good boyfriend material, then drop them for another challenge down the road. You're innocent of any cruel intention, but you're also not stupid; you know that you've hurt feelings.

The Moon in Sagittarius makes it easy for you to move on. This is the dark side of the sign. Love requires patience as well as staying power. You've heard the phrase "for better, for worse"? In your world, it's "for great times, then adios." You don't know how to handle it when someone else is in pain. You know how to keep your own pain to yourself and to keep moving so you don't feel it too long. So when someone interests you enough that you can tolerate his problems, you know you're halfway to love. You can be compassionate when you find that tolerant part of your inner self, and that's the part of you that's going to draw in true love.

It's one of life's little ironies: the stronger you are, the harder it is to be vulnerable. Your soft, quiet side—the one that you keep under wraps—is your ticket to emotional happiness.

So enjoy those days of catting about, and when

you're ready for a serious relationship, find the adventure between two people.

AstroBabe Planetary Pulse: 3
Sagittarius Moon Guy Planetary Pulse: 4

Moon in Capricorn

The Moon in the sign of Capricorn provides a careful, measured outward emotional state. Intuition can be strong when it's switched on, but it's not used often. This is because watery intuition and emotions are not easy to keep in check, something that doesn't suit this control-loving earth sign. Even if you're feeling hurt, you don't like to share it, and you also keep a tight fist when it comes to extending sympathy or empathy.

AstroBabes with the Moon in Capricorn are actually very provocative, especially to men who like the chase. You don't give over emotionally very easily, you don't go out of your way to make yourself available, and you don't give back a whole lot just because someone is giving over to you. It looks as if you don't care, but you do. Inside, you're soft and sensitive; you just don't want anyone to see that.

In love, AstroBabes with Moon in Capricorn are very loyal. While you keep your emotions under wraps, you still make your love known quietly, carefully, even subtly. You certainly don't give your heart away without great consideration. That guy has to earn it! He has to prove himself. Since you're very wary of being hurt, you're not going to be opening yourself too quickly.

The darker side of this Moon is, of course, going too far with all that aloof, self-protective energy. You can get so careful that you never take risks or allow yourself to meet and date someone who interests you. If you do get to that point, you can create too many obstacles or tests to find out if the guy is really worth your trouble. You tend to distance yourself from intimacy, not because you don't want it, but because it scares you.

There is a balance to be struck here. AstroBabes with Moon in Capricorn can be both mysterious *and* available. You can be with a guy without being totally vulnerable. Take it one step at a time. Go slowly. The right guy will be patient, and any guy who isn't patient isn't the right one.

There's no rushing an AstroBabe with Moon in Capricorn. You have to decide the right time and the right way to connect with the guy you want. Once you determine you're ready for a close relationship, you make it happen. You'll be amazed at how much fun it is to let your hair down and be yourself in every detail—even if you're not perfectly in control.

AstroBabe Planetary Pulse: 3

Capricorn Moon Guy Planetary Pulse: 3

Moon in Aquarius

The intuitive Moon placed in perceptive Aquarius makes an interesting combination. Being an air sign, Aquarius prefers to think through and consider emotions rather than feel them, and the inventive nature of the sign makes love seem impulsive and radical.

AstroBabes with the Moon in Aquarius like

interesting, unique, and even eccentric guys. You won't necessarily avoid conventional people or relationships, but you won't seek them out, either. Flirtations are easy; you can speak and read someone's mind at the same time, and you'll come off as easygoing and intelligent. You *are* very bright, of course, but easygoing . . . not so much. Aquarius is a fixed sign, and ultimately you'll reveal the fact that you're not as flexible as you seemed.

Aquarius is an electric, unpredictable sign. AstroBabes with Moon in Aquarius are emotionally hardwired for high-speed, long-distance connections but lack the tools for good old-fashioned, down-to-earth social chat. The idea of a guy is easier to handle than the guy himself. Being close to a guy requires being in sync with him, giving part of your control away. You can't "log off" when you're with someone else, although you may try, becoming cold and aloof. Let's face it—you're simply having a hard time trusting. The right guy will make you feel accepted for all of your eccentricities. Beware, though, a guy who doesn't inquire about your feelings. While being with someone as emotionally inaccessible as you are might feel comfortable at first, you won't be able to sustain a close relationship. There is such a thing as being too cool for your own good.

The best kind of love connection for you will be another free spirit, someone who enjoys sharing ideas and seeking interesting, new experiences, and who doesn't like to be tied down to routines. You'll also like a certain amount of constancy, though, because ultimately you're very loyal and trusting. Your best relationship will balance close ties with a great expanse of trust. Taking time together. and apart will be helpful.

Once you become aware of your unique desires and passions, you'll be able to connect with someone who matches you in the right way. You're not looking for a clone; you're looking for a complement. If you're the peanut butter, he's the jelly. You work well on your own *and* you make a delicious combination.

AstroBabe Planetary Pulse: 1
Aquarius Moon Guy Planetary Pulse: 2

Moon in Pisces

The Moon in Pisces is a fish in water, swimming in a hospitable element and allowing troubles to trickle off her back. Unlike the water signs of Cancer the Crab and Scorpio the Scorpion, Pisceans have no defense mechanisms with which to protect themselves. No hard shell, no poisonous tail, only gills that take in and expel everything around them. Because of this lack of barrier, Pisces is the most psychic sign of the zodiac. When you Pisceans use your intuition, you have access to all the knowledge around you, both hidden and open—others' thoughts, feelings, and intentions. Of course, this has a downside: TOO MUCH INFORMATION! Many people turn the power off and never use this great gift. In unpracticed hands, the power is too much.

Moon-in-Pisces AstroBabes are like no other. You have the ability to be both vulnerable and powerful at the same time. Vulnerability comes in the form of sensitivity and emotional attachment. Power is from the intelligence gathering you do on an unconscious basis. You sense what is going on beneath the surface and you take full advantage of it. While other signs are better at confrontation and battle, you are the one who moves quietly through turmoil, emerging unscathed and perhaps better off.

But to get to this point you have to learn some tough lessons. Pragmatism works when you're young—it may seem ruthless to others but it's natural to you. As you realize that your ability to sense your way through romance is effective, you'll also see that it happens to hurt others around you who are more direct in their methods. You could be seen as a "cold bitch" when all you're doing is swimming away from problems.

Your real path to finding true love is in your acceptance and use of your strong psychic gift. Romance has a better chance of bringing that deep, eternal love if you learn how to open your heart and soul. Once you are comfortable with your own talents, you'll meet someone who is equally as capable. He will share your dream of romantic utopia, but he will also live in the real world.

You have a great gift for love and it is yours to use.

You can bewitch, bedazzle, and bewilder to your heart's content.

AstroBabe Planetary Pulse: 4
Pisces Moon Guy Planetary Pulse: 3

FOUR

Mercury

Mercury is the planet that permits me to write this book, to know about astrology, to share it with you. Mercury is the planet of communication and, although you may not see how it can influence your sensual, sexual, or amorous connections, you need Mercury to connect you to the right guy. Unless you're into some very impersonal couplings, you must have some sort of communication in your relationships.

Mercury communication is not just about words, but is also about ideas, dreams, thoughts, inventions, understanding. Mercury makes your worldview unique, and allows you to share it with someone else. Mercury is whispers, body language, nuance, and hints. Mercury is teasing, joking, flirtation, and wisdom. Never underestimate the power of Mercury. It makes long-term relationships work and romance never less than interesting.

Mercury also works behind the scenes, linking you up to karmic situations throughout your life. If you happen to find someone who has Mercury in the exact placement of one of your own planets—that is, a conjunction—it means you've met this person before, and you have some karmic issues to work out or contracts to fulfill. You'll know these people right away. They seem like soul mates and they are in your life for a reason.

Mercury is a very adaptable planet. It takes on the characteristics of the sign it's in pretty easily. That means if your Mercury is in a sign that likes to communicate, you have a very easy time connecting to others. If your Mercury is in a sign that isn't so ready for expression, however, you won't be volunteering to write love letters or make speeches.

Not everyone has the gift of gab. Mercury performs its function differently in all twelve signs of the zodiac. Sometimes it's a quiet dreamer; sometimes it won't shut up. Mercury is going to reveal some astonishing information about your ability to connect, so pay attention, girls. Mercury has a lot to say.

AstroBabe Secrets of Mercury

If his Sun or Moon is in the same sign as your Mercury, you will understand each other without too much effort.

Mercury in Aries

Here's your catchphrase: "I am!" Mercury in Aries is strong-minded. When you get behind an idea, you can take it anywhere. You can be persuasive, even argumentative. But it's not about getting your own way (as others might perceive); it's because you really and truly believe in what you're saying. Look up the word "ardent" in the dictionary and you just might see your face.

There is no better teammate than someone with Mercury in Aries. You are exuberant, committed, excited. Your energy can be contagious. You're a natural cheerleader (if you're not on the field), a go-getter, a believer.

Mercury in Aries loves to read, to conquer new ideas, to have new information. You like new projects, to be at the frontier.

Given all this enthusiasm, you're an excellent date.

Here's the downside.

Aries is the sign of the self, and Mercury in Aries is very interested in self-exploration. This can border on self-obsession, as in, "Enough about me, what do *you* think of me?" Back to the phrase that describes Aries, "I am." If you find yourself saying "I" a lot when you're out on the prowl for romance, listen up! I know it's hard—often others don't have anything interesting to say. How often do you sit there bored to death? But you can't always carry the conversation. Take a few deep breaths and learn to listen with patience; you could actually learn something.

Mercury in Aries is also going to have stressful effects. Aries likes a challenge and with Mercury that means arguments (some for sport), conflicts, and changes of opinion. There are times when you'll leave in the morning with a strong opinion in one direction and come home with an equally strong opinion in the opposite one. Consistency is not part of your diet.

If you aren't gripped by some ardent, exuberant experience or belief, you can get bored, restless, and disorganized. You might stir up trouble to have something to do. Does that sound just the tiniest bit familiar?

Find the guy who keeps you interested on an intellectual level but won't be bullied into accepting all of your ideas, and you'll want to keep him.

AstroBabe Planetary Pulse: 1
Aries Mercury Guy Planetary Pulse: 3

Mercury in Taurus

Mercury, planet of communication and agility, in Taurus, a fixed earth sign—sounds like a tough match. How can a jumpy planet like that have any fun in a stable sign?

By listening. Mercury isn't just about spouting off information, you know; it's also about taking it in. Mercury loves to learn, and in Taurus, it gets a chance to shut up, sit down, and take a load off.

AstroBabes with Mercury in Taurus are the best listeners, a compelling and attractive quality. You really take in what someone else is saying. Astro-Babes know that guys like to talk, and being listened to makes a guy feel appreciated, valuable, and understood.

It's not that Mercury in Taurus doesn't talk, though. Of course you can express yourself. You choose your words carefully, and you have a gentle manner and tone. You can write well because you take time to listen to yourself and think through what you want to say.

So what's the Achilles' heel of Mercury in Taurus? You get the Couch Potato Prize. Yes, if you don't have a fascinating man to listen to, you have no problem just watching TV, listening to music, hanging out, and waiting for some entertainment. Mercury in Taurus can get a little sluggish (that's where the fixed earth energy takes over the zippy, peppy Mercury).

I know, I know. You're not cutting yourself off from the world; you can talk on the phone, IM a friend, and do pretty much anything on that couch. But watch how much time you're clocking there. Couch potatoes make poor AstroBabes. There's not a lot of allure and romance conjured on those cushions—well, maybe in your imagination ... but you want the real thing, right?

To get off the couch and back in the swing, allow your Mercury to take you outside for some recreation. Go to an art museum or a concert. Mercury in Taurus loves to take in beauty. You feed on ideas and the arts for your creativity and inspiration.

You'll meet a guy who has the same connection with the arts and with a cozy, at-home lifestyle. Together, you can design the home of your dreams and make that couch a place to plan your lives. But to find that romance, you have to get out there. There are plenty of guys who'd love to keep you company.

AstroBabe Planetary Pulse: 4
Taurus Mercury Guy Planetary Pulse: 2

Mercury in Gemini

Mercury, the planet that rules messages, communication, short trips, and quick studies, just adores the sign of Gemini. Here Mercury is able to shoot around the atmosphere without the confining force of a fixed or cardinal sign. Mercury is at home in Gemini and is therefore very powerful.

AstroBabes with Mercury in Gemini are chatty, smart, fun, and funny. You are excellent to hang around with because of your sense of humor and quick-on-the-draw mind. You can size up any situation and sum it up in one clever sentence. You generously share your insights and knowledge. You are easily inspired creatively and you enjoy being provoked by new ideas.

All this sharp Mercurial wit and energy is just great fun. But the mutability of the sign can make it hard to focus. There's so much of interest—so much to see, do, know, experience. Anyone who wants to be with you has to be able to keep up. He has to be smart, and smarter. And without hesitation this guy has to have a sense of humor. There is no way you can go out with someone who doesn't get your jokes. Not only does he have to get them and enjoy them, but he has to be able to make you laugh, too. In short, the two of you will have your own stand-up comedy thing going. Everyone will want you to come to their parties. No one will ever turn down your invitation, either.

As befits the sign of the Twins, there are two enemies of Mercury in Gemini. The first is boredom. You cannot sustain a strong relationship with anyone who bores you. Even if he makes you laugh, even if he gets your jokes, if he's not stimulating, he's out.

The second enemy is exhaustion. When you do find that perfect guy, you could both kill yourselves laughing. You don't know when to stop and take a break. In the beginning of a relationship, it's very easy to overdo. You'll both get so high on your mutual admiration and appreciation, you won't sleep much. As things settle down, learn to enjoy quieter times. You don't have to bring the house down with laughter or astound the world with your great wit every breathing moment.

If you can find the balance between zippety-zing and R and R, you'll have the perfect level of interest and magnetism to sustain your relationship.

AstroBabe Planetary Pulse: 5
Gemini Mercury Guy Planetary Pulse: 4

Mercury in Cancer

Not that there's a sign of the elephant in the zodiac, but if there were, it would exist for Mercury in Cancer. That's because elephants never forget and neither do you.

Mercury, the communicator, gets hunkered down into warm and cozy Cancer and sits there, taking notes on love and life. Don't even try to argue with me; you know it's true. You probably remember every kindness ever extended to you, and no doubt you have cataloged every cut, too. That's what Mercury in Cancer does best.

You're discreet, thank goodness, or everyone would know just how awful certain people are. You're also smart, reasonable, and sensitive. You tune in to music and poetry as if they were drugs, easing your soul and lifting your spirits.

In love and flirtation, you use your eyes more than words. You remember (of course) every date, anniversary, and moment of importance. It can be frustrating if he doesn't remember, but cut him slack—not everyone has a superglue memory like you.

You aren't always forthcoming when someone wants to get to know you. That's just your cautious way and it only increases your mystery and allure. Once you find a comfort level, you'll begin to open up. It's slow and steady, and you watch carefully for clues about how he's responding.

You are also immensely adaptable—on your own terms. When you decide he's worth it, you are able to shift and sway yourself to feel at home with him. This kind of Mercurial flexibility makes you a great mom as well as a great wife. Cancer just can't help it—this sign likes a serious relationship, so you'll find one sooner or later.

But back to being a girlfriend or date. You don't need to try hard at all—you're a natural. Go easy on the guy—not everyone has your memory! Be willing to open up slowly with your inner thoughts and feelings. And don't hold too many grudges—wouldn't you rather hold hands?

AstroBabe Planetary Pulse: 1
Cancer Mercury Guy Planetary Pulse: 1

Mercury in Leo

AstroBabes with Mercury in Leo are the idea leaders of the stars. You like to know, to share information, to understand new concepts and make them popular.

You can't help being entertaining—you possess a gift for interesting gab. You are determined and persistent, and aspire to your goals without fear.

Nothing like having an AstroBabe with Mercury in Leo at your dinner party. There are great jokes to tell, stories to share, new ideas to toss around. The planet of communication in the sign of entertainment and sports is great fun for games of all kinds with people of all ages.

So aside from being a great party favor, what is Mercury in Leo going to do for romance? It's great for flirting and for engaging in interesting conversation. You communicate with words as easily as with body language, and you don't leave anyone guessing. You know your mind and you put it out there clearly in an entertaining and endearing manner.

So what's the problem? The darker side of any Mercurial placement is where the words take over the feelings. If you fall over to the dark side, your words run away with you. In fact, that's hard to resist when you're talking about one of your pet ideas. It's not that you love to preach, but when you know more than others about something that means a lot to you, well, there's no keeping you from the podium. Take a breath once in a while and see if your audience is still interested. You can be especially difficult if you hit a topic that is emotionally charged and you feel strongly about it. Whether you're pro or con, liberal or conservative, you risk being a know-it-all windbag. Nothing takes the sweetness out of romance more than a narrow-minded dissertation on the World According to You. Remember to listen, honey. That's how you learn. Don't lose heart, dear Leo Mercury. You rarely venture into such passion-killing behavior.

Keep to your easy, charming ways. Enjoy sharing your ideas with others. You're so good at light romance and sweet talk, guys love it when you're around!

AstroBabe Planetary Pulse: 2
Leo Mercury Guy Planetary Pulse: 3

Mercury in Virgo

Being the zippy, fast-acting planet that it is, Mercury rules two signs. The first is Gemini, in which Mercury acts like Chatty Kathy. The second is Virgo, where Mercury inverts its energy to endow strong intuition, perception, and intellect. Mercury in Virgo has more answers, while Mercury in Gemini poses more questions. If you are an AstroBabe with Mercury in Virgo, you are blessed with a wonderful mind and an enormous capacity to understand both ideas and people.

This is not to say that you're bad at conversation—not in the least. You engage in charming conversation as well as provide persuasive arguments. You don't like silly banter as much as real discussion, but you can do both. You're probably more exacting than most of your friends, and it's hard to tone down that particular trait if you trade comments with a guy who isn't as smart as you. You don't really enjoy talking to someone who doesn't have something interesting to say.

Here's where we hit the more difficult side of Mercury in Virgo. You can be a little bit of a snob—the intellectual kind. It's important to remember that flirtation does not require a great brain. Engaging in light coquettish banter—or gestures—does not demand a great mind. You'll miss lighthearted, no-strings-attached fun if you insist on speaking only to those whose intellectual capacity is deep. There are plenty of people who are fascinating, provocative, and creative who are not what you'd call book smart.

When you decide to get serious about romance, you'll no doubt find a meeting of the minds. Preferably you'll get a guy who enjoys your organizational skills and wants to know what you really think about everything. It works best if he's smart in a different way than you are. That way you will learn from each other and be intrigued for a long time. Don't hook up with someone just because of his intelligence, though. You need passion, too. Words might caress your mind and imagination, but you should remember that, as an earth sign, you have even more fun when you communicate through touch.

AstroBabe Planetary Pulse: 4
Virgo Mercury Guy Planetary Pulse: 5

Mercury in Libra

Libra's influence on the planet of communication is interesting. Libra loves to learn and sort through knowledge to find both sides of the story. Mercury loves to learn and forge new territories. The combination makes for a strong mind, excellent intellectual faculties, and an easygoing attitude.

AstroBabes with Mercury in Libra are refined, beauty-loving, tender creatures who are oddly capable of being friendly without being warm. There is a coolness, an isolationist energy, in you simply because you have something on your mind, in your mind, or distracting your mind at all times. But everyone likes you and you are infinitely interesting and amusing, so what could be bad?

Mercury in Libra has a hard time making up its mind. Do you like this or that? Are you pro or con? Are you up or down? You can be both! Mercury is mutable and can take on either side of an argument. Libra is about balance and must understand both sides of an argument. Jumping from one side to another isn't uncommon. Now, apply this to your love life and you get—indecision.

Being a smart, good communicator is great, but when you find yourself agreeing with everyone and meaning it, you forget what you really think. It's hard to decide, too, because everyone makes such great points.

You can flirt, date, fall in love, and even marry but still feel on the fence about it all. It's not that you're not loyal or devoted, but you can't help examining all possibilities, all roads, whether or not you take them. No one ever knows, however, because you're truly discreet.

The best you can do is to keep your mind

occupied with matters that fulfill Libra's desire for beauty and harmony, such as art, music, books, and theater, and let your romantic wanderings take a backseat. Love the one you're with. When you feel, rather than *think* about it, you probably made the right decision.

In the event that you have to choose between two guys, use your gut. Do not fall into that intellectual ambivalence. They'll both get bored waiting for the outcome.

AstroBabe Planetary Pulse: 2
Libra Mercury Guy Planetary Pulse: 4

Mercury in Scorpio

Mercury finds a deep and creative home in the sign of Scorpio. The intensity of the sign, its creativity and focus, give Mercury a fertile ground in which to investigate, understand, and synthesize. Mercury loses some of its agitation here, and settles down to study, think, and create. However, once in a while the planet rears into spontaneity, and you never know what clever or biting comments might emerge.

Since Scorpio is a sign that prefers to go inward rather than outward, most of the time Mercury keeps communication measured and cautious. Privacy and keeping secrets are actually possible when Mercury is in this more silent sign. AstroBabes with Mercury in Scorpio can be very internal, and most certainly very smart. But who can know what's going on in that head of yours? You have to tell us at some point.

All too often, Mercury in Scorpio causes Astro-Babes to use sarcasm. It's always clever and often funny, but you use it for distancing yourself instead of drawing people closer. No one wants to get stung twice by the Scorpion's tongue—it's almost as painful as its tail. Plus, you're not a forgiving type. If a guy threatens you, you prefer to keep him on your private blacklist.

However, when you do choose to be, you are the best friend and most devoted lover imaginable. You're amazing and wonderful to those you love, and scary and harsh to those you disdain.

So AstroBabes with Mercury in Scorpio must learn to keep their counsel, hold their tongues in moments of stress. Use that intelligence and fortitude to figure out a better moment and better words to express your anger, your dissatisfaction, or your problems instead of reducing someone to ashes.

By the way, you aren't so resilient yourself, honey, so don't dish out what you don't want to take. Use your power wisely and you will enjoy a scintillating, deeply connected relationship that respects your comfort levels and diminishes the power of your secrets.

AstroBabe Planetary Pulse: 1
Scorpio Mercury Guy Planetary Pulse: 1

Mercury in Sagittarius

Put one chatty planet in the sign that loves to learn and you get a very knowledgeable, smart, and talkative person. Since Mercury is a shifty planet and Sagittarius is mutable, there are no bounds to the mind of this AstroBabe. Most of her knowledge will stick, so a lifetime of learning is available at any given moment.

If you are an AstroBabe with Mercury in Sagittarius, you are no shrinking violet. You can talk to anyone, anywhere, about almost anything. Since you have a magnetic mind, you grasp new ideas and information quickly. You're a lively conversationalist and a whiz at parties. Flirting is easier for you than for most, but you're not always on the flirt level. Sometimes you just like to talk to share ideas.

The dark side of Mercury in Sagittarius is the extreme end of the spectrum. All talking, lecturing, pontificating. No one likes to be lectured, least of all your friends or guys who are interested in romance. You will miss many cues if you get too caught up in your subject matter and not in the audience. Not that you're boring, but not everyone wants to learn something at a party or an outing, or when just hanging out. When in doubt, let someone else talk. See what happens—does the subject change? Does anyone want to do something else? Tune in to the group so they don't tune you out.

Of course, when a Mercury-in-Sagittarius Astro-Babe decides that romance is her game, she's a great player. You can shift and turn and twirl your words and gestures to interest just about any guy. But your guy has to be smart, tolerant, game for new ideas, and interesting. You aren't going to love someone who doesn't let you speak freely and who doesn't have a sense of humor.

He also has to be honest and principled, because you can't stand corrupt or lazy sensibilities. Once you make up your mind that you like him, you're staunch; once you decide he's the right guy, he is. Even though you possess mutable energy, your mind is irrefutable. You know what you know and that's the end of the story. If you pick a guy who is as smart and energetic as you are, the story does indeed have a happy ending.

AstroBabe Planetary Pulse: 3
Sagittarius Mercury Guy Planetary Pulse: 2

Mercury in Capricorn

Mercury, the energetic planet of communication and journeys, lands in Capricorn and becomes acquainted with focus, direction, and achievement. Instead of flitting about trading little pieces of information, Mercury settles down to absorb information and opinion, to consider concepts and ideals. Still able to conjure a sense of humor, Mercury isn't completely serious. But here in Capricorn, Mercury does appreciate getting down to business.

For you AstroBabes with Mercury in Capricorn, this means pleasures in an intellectual realm. It's not that you need to read big books or earn PhDs in history. You just prefer people, men especially, who have lived and experienced more than you have. You like to listen, to learn from them. And when you feel prepared, you speak up, typically with authority. You have to feel as if what you say is solid before you share, and your manner is both persuasive and poised.

As you might expect, AstroBabes with Mercury in Capricorn are not the biggest flirts at the frat party. You do very well, however, at cocktail parties and other grown-up social affairs. You know how to keep your own counsel if you aren't versed in the subject at hand, but you can appear very intelligent and forthright when you are in the know.

So what's the downside? You worry a lot. ("What do I know?") You don't have an easy connection with lighthearted banter. Your natural penchant for real knowledge keeps you from some kinds of silliness that others enjoy. Perhaps potty humor isn't your thing.

Of course, it takes time to connect with a guy whom you respect and who respects you. You're likely to prefer guys who are older and wiser, at least in appearance. It might take time to find the guy who is both mature and accepting enough to put you on his level. You might try a few father figures before you get to the guy who can be your equal. And you'll learn that older does *not* always mean wiser!

However you do get there, your love life will be multilayered, with intellectual connections as well as passion and fun. You wait for the right match, even if it looks like you'll never find it. But of course, you do. Mercury in Capricorn never settles for less.

AstroBabe Planetary Pulse: 3
Capricorn Mercury Guy Planetary Pulse: 3

Mercury in Aquarius

Communication- and information-loving Mercury finds a pleasant environment in the inventive and perceptive sign of Aquarius. This is a mutually beneficial relationship, where Mercury is stabilized by the fixed energy of the sign but is able to enjoy a great expanse in the realm of thought, especially invention and creativity.

AstroBabes with Mercury in Aquarius are wonderfully interesting, smart, and insightful. You're constantly receiving intuitive information, which makes you an excellent people reader. With guys, you can use this to flirt and converse without effort. You have a natural magnetism simply standing alone, saying nothing, but you won't be alone for long. You'll always draw guys to you, and it will be your job to figure out who's worth your while.

Although you're very perceptive, you don't always listen to your instincts. It's tempting to turn off that inner voice and just deal with people on a surface level. This, of course, will always get you into trouble. You cannot expect a life full of people discussing the latest TV shows or sports phenoms to keep you happy. Your interest can be held only for so long before you look for a wall to climb. Face it—you're not the one people come to for the latest joke or advice on fashion. You simply don't care that much. Mercury in Aquarius is a psychic placement, and you're a Babe who can be drawn to investigating astrology, tarot, and healing arts. As you get older, these interests will become second nature and nothing will seem too extraordinary. You're naturally hooked up to divine information and you'll always be able to use it.

In romance, a guy who will connect well with you must be intelligent and accepting. He won't be scared off by your sixth sense nor will he judge your intense hunches and sudden perceptions. Even if he's a conventional guy with a "normal" job, he won't feel staid or limiting to you. You'll be connected on a deeper level and find the place where you share values and principles.

Give any new relationship a chance to settle and shift into a comfort zone and find that place of connection. If you do find a guy whose inner self makes perfect sense to you, you'll have an enduring, interesting, and evolving relationship.

AstroBabe Planetary Pulse: 4
Aquarius Mercury Guy Planetary Pulse: 4

Mercury in Pisces

Watery, dreamy Pisces and the eager-to-communicate planet of Mercury combine to make, yes, great poetry. Flippant, agile Mercury dives through many depths of Pisces exploring romantic, passionate, and intensely creative expression. Great art and ideas are born from this placement.

Music, art, poetry, and romantic films are all in the domain of Mercury in Pisces. AstroBabes with this Mercury have the ability to float to a new level of reality—or at least it seems that way. You are great appreciators as well as great creators. Your mind adventures through the realms of spirit and creativity to find beauty and pleasure. In short, you tend toward escapism.

In romance, there are two roads. Either you love

to talk and share, or you're the listener, the one who allows others to unload their secrets. The chatty AstroBabes are better flirts. Listeners find a lot of guys who are interested in them but few who turn their heads. All Pisces Mercury AstroBabes have a vision, usually indescribable, of the guy who will be The One. He is sensitive, without a doubt. He is romantic, like you, and he is not averse to giving or receiving a massage. Your type of guy can be any sign, but he has to have a clear head and a true heart.

Your romantic notions will mature over time, and what was once your dream date—a picnic with wine and cheese—will evolve into a desire for music, dancing, and elegant dinners. Your romantic streak grows more sophisticated and sometimes more out of reach.

Music is one constant in your life that will bring you pleasure and passion. Your guy will be into your tunes and you'll be into his. Music can be used to create the romantic atmosphere you crave as well as soothe feelings when you're stressed or angry.

A guy who likes to dip into your romantic and passionate fantasies will be your dream come true.

But make sure he's a practical person when it comes to everyday life. You don't want to date a ditz.

AstroBabe Planetary Pulse: 4
Pisces Mercury Guy Planetary Pulse: 2

FIVE

Venus

AstroBabes, here it is, your best friend in the zodiac. Venus is the all-purpose happy planet, the ruler of love, money, beauty, and all gentle and refined pursuits. We love Venus. Venus loves us.

Venus reigns over the home, decoration, luxury, and a sense of harmony. Venus is the female planet that unites with its male counterpart, Mars, for passionate play. Ruling touch and sensual pleasures, Venus is a very important planet to understand and enjoy. She likes to be indulged. Don't *you*?

Venus is helpful in all aspects of love. It's the planet that makes you lovely, loving, and lovable.

Venus operates well in all signs and brings you your own special loving assets.

Can there possibly be a downside to Venus? It's hard to imagine, but yes, you do have to be cautious when it comes to the pleasure-seeking and pleasure-loving side of this planet. There *can* be too much of a good thing. Venus likes to lean into bliss, to lilt into dreamy perfection. That's where the trouble starts. There are times when Venus will compel you to deny some of the harder edges of life. Venus can also be overindulgent, egging you on in eating, drinking, even drug taking, for the momentary pleasures they bring. You have to know when Venus is leaning a little too heavily on the pleasure button and it's time to get back to work.

Wherever your Venus is in your chart, get to know the little nuances she brings to your romantic life. In fire signs she provides passionate engagement; in earth signs it's sensual pleasures and a propensity to receive gifts(!); in air signs you'll love a meeting of the romantic and flirtatious minds; and in water signs it's all about under-the-radar emotional connection. Every single one of these Venus signs can get carried away, so be warned. Too much of a good thing can have consequences in other parts of your life. Venus can lead you to success as well as love, but she can't have the last word. Let Venus work with the Sun, the Moon, Mercury, and Mars, and you'll be one amazing AstroBabe.

AstroBabe Secret of Venus

If your Venus and his Mars are in the same sign, passion will be easy and natural.

Venus in Aries

If Venus shares its gifts with you in the fiery, take-charge sign of Aries, you have a lot of energy for love. You yearn to be ignited by the fires of passion. You thirst for the chase, the thrills, the excitement. The problem is, you also like your independence.

First, there are a lot of qualities that help Astro-Babes with Venus in Aries pursue romance and love. You're not afraid of it, so that's already a big step.

You have the ability to truly love yourself, and that's even better. Good self-esteem is the must-have of all happy love relationships.

Venus in Aries also has a lot of energy. Physical workouts and outdoor activities are excellent places to spend untapped passion and even meet potential romantic interests. You're also not afraid of competition, and a challenge, romantic or otherwise, is a welcome addition to your life.

So what to do with all that love and energy, all that verve and lust for life?

Look for someone just like you.

Venus in Aries needs a companion who gets how you operate. Aries is a tricky sign for partnership because it rules the self, the very essence of independence. You won't feel so inclined to find a boyfriend in every phase of your life. You're not one of those girls who wants or needs a companion every second. Your independence is very attractive to guys, but you do have to find a way to include someone else in your life when you want to get serious. Otherwise you won't ever settle down.

Venus always has its dark side, and in Aries it's about sharing. Being competitive can make it hard to be in a partnership; Venus here is always trying to outdo someone. Being happy with yourself can become, in its extreme, self-involved and egocentric. You might not attract anyone else if you're perceived to be completely happy on your own. The image may not be true, but you'll have to work on letting others know you'd like to find some romance.

Look to your other planets for help if Venus in Aries seems to keep you solo. Your Moon can soften the militant Venus and coax it to settle down and enjoy softer pursuits. Your Mars, too, might want to find a way to engage in love with a little sizzling give-and-take.

AstroBabe Planetary Pulse: 1
Aries Venus Guy Planetary Pulse: 2

Venus in Taurus

At home in Taurus, Venus reclines with all the beauty and serenity in the world. AstroBabes with Venus in Taurus have a strong connection to all that is feminine and physical.

Gardens, art, beautiful things, beautiful people—that's what you like. Venus in Taurus is an excellent girlfriend and a great lover. What can be bad?

The Taurus influence over Venus makes money and property a pretty big deal. In a word, you can be possessive. You want to hold on to what you have and possibly acquire more. "To have and to hold" is a serious declaration for you. Lighthearted, light-handed romance isn't your thing. Flings aren't the least bit satisfying.

Venus in Taurus is also naïve. You are lovely, but vulnerable, a very attractive quality to most guys. Your gentle energy creates a happy aura, ready to engage with others. You trust nice people. Sometimes you trust the wrong guys. AstroBabes with Venus in Taurus will typically have one or two relationships that start out with great promise and end up far from paradise. You get yourself into those messes so you can learn about the darker side of relationships.

Given the opportunity, Venus in Taurus would happily see only the best in people and the most beautiful parts of life, and wander down the path of least resistance. That's why life is going to dish out some spicy obstacles. It's the only way you'll learn!

Relationships benefit from your natural inclination for loyalty, but when they're over, you find it hard to let go. Venus in Taurus always needs a push to move on. It's not that it's ever hard to find new romance; it's just such a bother.

But not to worry. Once you get a little wiser in the world, you will have a wonderful, gentle, loving relationship that lasts. You'll prefer a guy who makes a good living, who offers security, and whom you can trust. Ultimately, you will enjoy being a homebody, surrounded by your beautiful things and your loving family.

AstroBabe Planetary Pulse: 5
Taurus Venus Guy Planetary Pulse: 4

Venus in Gemini

The loving, girlie planet Venus finds itself in airy, mutable Gemini and realizes the delights of breezy conversation, new ideas, and fun, fun, fun. Venus finds it easy to enjoy wit, humor, chat, and gossip. Truth be told, Venus loves a good tidbit to jaw on with her girlfriends.

So AstroBabes with Venus in Gemini are, of course, wonderful flirts. You play with words; you loll in ideas, fantasies, fiction, and poetry. You like a guy who can talk, but you love a guy who has an amazing mind. Your passion is the intellect. Whoever said that the brain was the most important sex organ was talking about you. Any guy who turns *you* on is bound to be interesting.

And here's the thing. You can't pass up a chance to talk to someone who strikes you as interesting. You just have to find out what's going on in his mind, even if it means that your date or your boyfriend gets a little annoyed! You still have to satisfy your curiosity. Some call you fickle, but you know that you're just compelled to dig. The girl's gotta have it!

The influence of Gemini (the Twins) can compel Venus to find more than one source of pleasure, more than one love interest. I can see all you hip, young AstroBabes nodding along and even smiling knowingly. But you AstroBabes who are old enough to know better should not be smiling—not if you want to have a long-term relationship. Remember, Venus can be swayed by sensuous pleasure, fleeting as it might be, but when you're grown-up and into more serious relationships, you'd better know when to say no to these impulses. Venus can be just as easily amused by good conversation.

Like most planets in Gemini, Venus would like to make a love match of the minds. You can't allow your relationship to get dumbed down and you can't stay with someone who doesn't continue to grow, seek, learn, and share. No strong, silent types for you.

Look for a guy who knows how to communicate beyond storytelling and lecturing. You need someone who can articulate his feelings and keep you interested! And it's up to you to focus, pal.

AstroBabe Planetary Pulse: 2
Gemini Venus Guy Planetary Pulse: 2

Venus in Cancer

Venus, the all-purpose planet of love, and Cancer, the sign of the mother and the home, is a match made in heaven. You AstroBabes with this combination are the emotional center for your family and friends. You get a lot of love, you thrive on love— and you learn from love.

Venus in Cancer is very loyal and devoted. Loyalty has two sides, as you may already know. There is the loyalty that stands by a loved one through difficult times, making the relationship closer and stronger, and there's the loyalty that stays with a loved one even though the relationship is over or the situation demands moving on. Venus in Cancer will stick it out for better or worse but sometimes the worse ... isn't worth it. When it's over, the faster you move on, the faster you'll find new, better love.

Because your Venus sign is family-loving Cancer, family loyalties can seem more important than having your own love life. To excel as an AstroBabe, you have to make a real effort and get out there. The good news is that you'll find you enjoy being "out there." You'll like the adventure (in measured doses), and you'll really enjoy the friendships you establish that make the outside world more like inside family! With Venus in Cancer, everyone you like is eventually treated like family.

In dating, you'll attract guys who appreciate your loyalty and deserve your devotion. You will, however, also get your fair share of the kind who love your devotion but do nothing to deserve it. You do have keen intuition, but you're not infallible. You might be swayed by a few great dates and sweet words only to discover that the guy's a jerk, and that he's fickle. That kind of guy will not do at all. These are among the many lessons you'll get in love.

AstroBabes with Venus in Cancer do typically find someone who is worthy of devotion and who likes a cozy place to live. You'll be the AstroBabe who entertains at home more and more. Your gentle energy is much loved and always needed. Share it with those who can respect how much you care.

AstroBabe Planetary Pulse: 3
Cancer Venus Guy Planetary Pulse: 4

Venus in Leo

Woo-hoo! Lucky you, you've got the planet of love in the sign of the Sun, two positive and joy-producing energies combined to make sure good times are had by all. You have a big heart, a large capacity for love, and an unending supply of social acumen.

First things first. You are one of the best flirts on the planet. You love to wink, gaze, chat, dance, entertain, lead, and let yourself be led. Flirtation is a sport and you are a top-ranked player.

You have no problem attracting guys. There are plenty around who will engage in your games, and when you want to get serious, you can have your pick. It's hard to get serious right away, though, when you're an AstroBabe with Venus in Leo. You like to have fun and that's what you should be having. You won't stick around for complicated, difficult relationships when you're young. How can you miss all that fun stuff? Working on relationships is a waste of precious time. You'll save that for when you're really ready to settle down.

You like a guy who knows how to have a good time and who isn't afraid to take risks, someone accomplished, sure of himself and goal oriented.

But not only does this guy have to be game; he has to be able to afford you! When Venus in Leo leans a little too hard on the pleasure button, you can be high maintenance. Come on, this is not exactly a shock. You can be a present-loving, good-restaurant-going, jewelry-sporting, high-heeled Babe. You have to watch the material side of Venus if you find that diamonds and gold are all you think about. Sure, it's okay if he spends money on you, but it can't be the single most important criterion of your love affair. Money doesn't buy passion, connection, and fun—you two have to find those together.

Sure, he's got to be fun, but you've got to keep your feet on the ground. He's not an *accessory*; he's a human being.

Attention, Venus-in-Leo AstroBabes: enjoy your gifts of beauty, love, and happiness. Share your warm heart and joyful spirit with all of us. Accept those gifts that you are so generously offered, but don't forget that you, too, are a mere mortal.

AstroBabe Planetary Pulse: 4
Leo Venus Guy Planetary Pulse: 4

Venus in Virgo

With her love of beauty and order, Venus settles into Virgo calmly. An AstroBabe with this planet-sign combination enjoys organizing her household, her friends, her life, with a gentle hand and deep affection for art and comfort. Here Venus sets aside her tendency toward giddiness in favor of the no-nonsense quality that Virgo prefers, but finds pleasure in different ways.

You AstroBabes with Venus in Virgo are known for your particular tastes. If friends call you picky, you won't be quick to deny it. Clothes, jobs, apartments, shoes, whatever it is, you choose only what appeals to you even if no one else understands your choice.

With guys, too, you take your time. You wait for the right one, but your friends might scratch their heads, wondering why you picked him. You see beyond social and class barriers. You could date a street vendor or an industrial magnate—it's not a matter of what he does but what his heart is like. You know a good heart, a kind person, a true soul, when you see him. And to your credit, you usually end up with a great guy.

And the dark side? You're a sucker for a wounded heart, a sick puppy, a guy who *needs* you (at least you *think* he needs you). You love to nurture, and if you sense someone in pain, you'll run to fix it. It can get unpleasant when he doesn't want to be taken care of, or you get tired of pouring your energy into his life without any satisfaction . . . even worse, if he gets over his wounds and moves on to someone else. You'll end up with one or two guys like this because Venus will lead you to them for this lesson in love. When you do realize that this guy isn't worthy of you, get out.

In all, AstroBabes with Venus in Virgo have wonderfully loving hearts. Once you find a man who is actually worthy of your kindness and who appreciates all you have to offer, you will indeed live happily ever after.

AstroBabe Planetary Pulse: 2
Virgo Venus Guy Planetary Pulse: 3

Venus in Libra

Like Mercury, Venus has two homes in the zodiac. After all, there are so many ways to imbue the world with beauty. In Taurus, Venus is about physical beauty; in Libra, it's about the realm of ideas, ideals, art. The idea of being in love, loving someone else, being loved in return—this is a matter for Venus in Libra.

AstroBabes with Venus in Libra are very aesthetic. You are beautiful yourself, of course, and you prefer others to be good-looking, too. You are very flirtatious—it's hard not to be when Venus takes over and keeps your charisma strong. You are also kind. You take care not to hurt others, and you keep things light and agreeable for everyone around you, even those who are much less talented in the art of love.

Venus in Libra tunes in to beauty through music, art, literature, poetry, dance—all that can layer any occasion or location with harmony. You naturally gravitate to places that are peaceful as well as use your sixth sense to avoid people and situations that aren't in sync with your need for balance. Translated, this roughly means you hate conflict. You avoid unpleasant places and experiences even if it means you indirectly suffer for it. You won't take on a problem if the people involved are rough and tough. You won't go to a dinner party if the setting is dour and depressing. It takes a lot to coax you into less-than-perfect circumstances.

And that leads you to the darker side of Venus in Libra. You want beauty and peace all around you, but love, at least romantic love, is not always a bed of roses. You'd like to believe in perfect love, but that isn't reality. Venus in Libra can keep you from developing a deep relationship by making you reluctant to stray outside of your harmonious zones. Remember that true love runs beneath the surface. Relationships can be gritty; they most certainly contain disagreements, which are not pretty. Once you pass through the unpleasantness, however, you'll find the core beauty of your shared love. That's what it's all about.

AstroBabes with Venus in Libra must face conflict and imperfection, fighting the superficial in order to reach the beauty beneath the surface of a good, strong love connection.

AstroBabe Planetary Pulse: 5
Libra Venus Guy Planetary Pulse: 5

Venus in Scorpio

Loving, sexy Venus finds a lot of opportunities to excel in intense and powerful Scorpio. Venus demands pleasure and creating opportunities for good times, and uses the force and energy of Scorpio to meet its goals. AstroBabes with Venus in Scorpio know what I mean.

Since Scorpio is private and prefers controlled circumstances, Venus in Scorpio plays it low-key in public. You AstroBabes with Venus in Scorpio won't publicize your inner passion or even the guy this passion's all about. Don't be surprised if you tend toward secret love affairs—you feel more in control when fewer people know. But secret love affairs don't fulfill you completely and you'll soon tire of them.

Ultimately, you need to express your passion. You have an enormous inner life. You spend more time by yourself than most. And that needs connection. But since you don't like to be vulnerable, you tend to avoid showing yourself to those you don't know (you even keep secrets from people you do know!). Once you find the guy you feel even a little comfortable with, try to show him the real you. Go slowly, carefully, so that you don't get scared. The more he knows you, the more you'll trust him and allow that amazing passion to come alive.

The dark side of Venus in Scorpio is its desire for control. Keeping secrets, being possessive or jealous, assessing his wealth before his heart—this is Venus being interested more in her own pleasure than in being true to you and your search for true love. When you're young, you'll be tempted to experiment with forbidden pleasures—drugs, sexual encounters, secret affairs, whatever is enticing and withheld from you. As you get older, you must emerge from creating illicit or short-lived pleasures so that you can create those that will fulfill you for the long term. Venus in Scorpio likes to induce feelings of bliss, and this can mean problems with drugs or alcohol. Again, don't go too far here, because it's easy to get hooked.

Don't be afraid to express the passion of your Venus, but be in control of it. In a relationship, use it to unleash powerful sexual energy and weave an impenetrable bond between you and your guy. He'll be thrilled—and faithful!

AstroBabe Planetary Pulse: 3
Scorpio Venus Guy Planetary Pulse: 3

Venus in Sagittarius

Energetic and adventurous Sagittarius embraces Venus in all her beauty and love, and makes you an excellent, exuberant AstroBabe. Since Venus finds beauty and harmony wherever she goes, Sagittarius opens doors to new pleasure and thrills. This is not a stay-at-home Venus sign. This is a get-out-there-and-live-to-the-limit combination.

AstroBabes with Venus in Sagittarius like the great outdoors. Let's go up that mountain or down that trail. Let's skate or ski, swim or sail. Let's do something! You'd be hard put to find a couch potato with this planetary placement.

Mutable Sagittarius and pleasure-seeking Venus create a get-up-and-go-for-it kind of energy. Forget boredom—the word isn't in your vocabulary (or you leave before it can happen). You're the first one in line to try the latest roller coaster, and your response to guys isn't much different. If he's cool, interesting, and active, he's someone you'll look at. But the next guy comes along with a different tune—maybe a different kind of interesting—and your head turns. Honey, it's not that you can't find someone to go out with; it's that you have to stick to him. One guy, get it?

It takes more than a few flubbed relationships to get the lesson down. You won't have intimacy without being deeply honest and tolerant of someone else, and that means staying put long enough to feel that depth. You won't find a great relationship while you're a moving target, so you have to keep your impulse to mountain climb (or whatever it is) in check even if you think you're bored (you're not bored—you're just being uncreative).

Don't worry—AstroBabes with this placement of Venus are fully capable of conjuring happiness. You can and will fulfill your romantic dreams when you have the time and patience to do so. In fact you will find that there is enormous adventure in a committed relationship. Love is an indoor-outdoor sport!

You must learn to stay still long enough to feel something deeply and to express yourself in matters of love. It's not that you're insincere or shallow; you're simply not that interested in introspection and articulating your feelings. But the right guy is going to be deeply interested in all of you—so get used to it.

AstroBabe Planetary Pulse: 3
Sagittarius Venus Guy Planetary Pulse: 3

Venus in Capricorn

Lovely, lilting, pleasure-seeking Venus lands in grounded, earnest Capricorn and looks around wondering how to please herself. It's not hard! With the energy and ambition of cardinal Capricorn ready to achieve its goals, Venus, maker of harmony and beauty, is able to get exactly what she wants. Of course.

AstroBabes with Venus in Capricorn possess a strong desire to acquire beautiful things, good men, nice homes, basically anything of quality and value. You are discerning, but that's not news to you. Your good taste is embedded in your nature. There's no bargaining down with you. You pay for quality and you expect to have it.

This isn't to say that you have to have a lot of stuff. AstroBabes with Venus in Capricorn are far happier with one very good piece of furniture than a room full of mediocrity. You seek quality, not quantity, and value, not economy.

Venus in Capricorn pushes to get the best in

everything. In love, this Venus has a hard time separating the guy from his social position, his intellect, and his taste for the finer things. He doesn't have to be rich or powerful, but it sure helps. You don't even notice this, because the very things you want are like magnets. Blindfolded and presented with a choice between two men, you'd choose the one who emanated the most power.

As for the weaker side of Venus in Capricorn, you could look like you only go for guys with hot cars or big jobs. You're also used to playing it cool (this is what those guys like, right?). But coolness isn't going to allow you to be wildly in love. For Venus in Capricorn, love feels a little reckless; "falling" in love is out of control!

In romance, you're careful. You're slow to start. Even if your girlfriends are going out every night, you're happy to stay home unless there's a guy who meets your standards. You're not a snob; you're just a girl who chooses carefully and, most often, wisely.

You need to find the right guy and when you do, let it rip—show your true feelings without worrying about how you look or what he's thinking. He's going to love it all.

AstroBabe Planetary Pulse: 3
Capricorn Venus Guy Planetary Pulse: 3

Venus in Aquarius

Loving, artistic, and beautiful Venus finds great expanse in Aquarius, the sign of hopes and wishes, friendships and humanitarian principles. In this fixed air sign, Venus isn't as materialistic or self-interested as it is in other signs. Rather, ideas, inventions, new ways to make the world a better place keep Venus busy and happy.

AstroBabes with Venus in Aquarius are idealistic and have great imaginations. Venus here gives over to potential, to creating—at least in the mind—what life could be and should be.

In love, Venus in independence-loving Aquarius does give out mixed signals. Even though you don't need anyone, that doesn't mean you don't want anyone. You don't want just any guy, though. There's a lot to do and to learn in life, and you don't want to give up your freedom for a relationship that might limit what you can do. That's why love has to sneak up on you to get through. You'll avoid it if you see it coming.

What is most important to you is finding someone who is accepting of you and your attitude and values. Anyone who harbors a great deal of judgment or lives by strict rules can't work with you. You don't like social-class lines in your life, and any guy who wants to be with you can't abide them, either.

While you don't actively seek romance or desire it on the same level as AstroBabes with other placements of Venus, love is not out of the question. Tend to your interests, enjoy the arts, culture, reading, theater, and you'll find guys who are like-minded. No doubt you'll enjoy a few relationships with people your friends think are weird (which is, of course, precisely why you like them!).

The challenge to AstroBabes with Venus in Aquarius is letting love happen and evolve in a natural, deeply connected way. You may not have the patience to wade through someone else's life. You might feel that your friends are enough to keep you busy and happy, so why bother to pursue romance, which may or may not be fun? Here's why: while it's true that you don't need to be in love, love will open your life in new ways.

Love teaches you how to feel. It puts you in touch with deeper creativity and even stronger intuition. The upside of exploring love is irresistible when you think about it.

You can pursue more of what you want from life when you go through it with someone else.

Ultimately, a guy you'll fall for will be the one who "gets" you without having to ask questions. Your wavelengths will match perfectly. Be patient. You don't have to have the whole love thing sorted out by next Tuesday or even next year. AstroBabes with Venus in Aquarius like to take their time, letting love find them at whatever age they choose.

AstroBabe Planetary Pulse: 3
Aquarius Venus Guy Planetary Pulse: 2

Venus in Pisces

The combination of the planet Venus and the sign of Pisces is a match made in, well, heaven. Venus loves love, loves luxury, loves beauty, loves pleasure. Pisces is seeking eternal, infinite bliss. It's definitely a potent combination, but as with good wine or fine chocolate, there can be too much of a good thing.

AstroBabes with Venus in Pisces are bliss-seeking missiles. Yet your ideals of love are so strong that it is often a substantial matter of time before you allow real love to take root. So many other things give pleasure—family, food, drink, friends, art, music, the outdoors, and so on. You have plenty of fantasies about love at any given moment, but it can take you a lot of time to get real.

With all this romantic potential, the AstroBabe with Venus in Pisces is a great girlfriend and wife. Guys with more adventurous, fleeting notions of romance need not apply. AstroBabes with Venus here want the real thing: love, marriage, children. And there's not a single doubt that you'll be a great mom, a great lover, a great nurturer. You only have to find the right guy, a die-hard romantic in a killer bod (or a reasonable facsimile).

The trouble for Venus in Pisces is that it wants only pleasure. You don't like facing the less pleasant sides of reality. Fights are to be avoided; suspicions are to be withheld. This lack of fortitude can land you in serious trouble. Too much of this sidestepping and you'll be a paranoid isolationist— hardly a success in love. You have to cut yourself and the world a break by trusting that you're not going to be annihilated by standing up for what you want. Facing "ugliness" only gets you back to beauty faster.

Impracticality also plagues AstroBabes with Venus in Pisces. You can see how wonderful things *can* be—but you're not so strong on how that can really happen. As much as fairy godmothers are in demand, there are few to spare. Dealing in reality is better. Take off those rose-colored glasses so that you can make your dreams come true here on earth.

Never stop dreaming, but don't avoid living. Love can be found and enjoyed without having to paint too many fake flourishes, and rough times aren't as miserable and enduring as you think.

AstroBabe Planetary Pulse: 5
Pisces Venus Guy Planetary Pulse: 3

SIX

Mars

What is the god of war doing·in a book about romance? He's here holding up his team, that is, the guys. Mars rules men, not just war. Mars also makes its energy available to work, passion, and hard recreation. Mars rules ambitions and desires, both qualities that are welcome and useful in the world of romance. It also rules strength and courage. Mars may not be everyone's dream of a romantic companion, but we all need a little of its energy to keep up the passionate part of life.

Mars works differently in each element. The ruler of Aries, Mars is most comfortable in the fire signs, where it moves with purpose and strength.

Someone with Mars in a fire sign loves new experiences and social situations. You won't find this person easily intimidated, but on the downside, a lot of pride and competitiveness is involved with Mars in this element. Watch for aggression, impatience, and a little too much competitive drive.

Mars in earth signs is less aggressive and more interested in physical stuff than in experiences. This Mars likes to spend money, to acquire new things, to express its energy in personal ambition, and to work hard to achieve more. People with Mars in earth signs also like food. Cooking might be the way to the Mars-in-earth-sign heart!

AstroBabes with Mars in air signs like banter, discussion, arguments, new ideas, concepts; they are ardent lecturers, they like to learn, and there may be some interest in intellectual games. The term "strong-minded" is associated with Mars in an air sign, as well as "impulsive," "argumentative," and "critical."

In water signs, Mars is like a guy buying tampons. He has a reason and a right to buy them, but he's clearly not comfortable with the whole task. Mars is the fiery go-getter, and he's got to express his passion without getting doused by watery emotion. On the upside, Mars can make water steamy (great for total abandon), and when it's right, Mars puts a lot of energy into commitment. While water is not an easy element for Mars, it is always interesting.

AstroBabe Secret of Mars

If his Mars is near your Moon, you might be sensitive to the way he expresses his anger.

Mars in Aries

At home in Aries, active and purposeful, Mars is in its element. Here, the combat-prone planet is looking for action in every part of life. For AstroBabes, this placement requires some careful balance.

Mars is into war. Whereas Venus loves to love, Mars thirsts for challenge. If you have Mars in Aries, this mean you like to pursue. You like the energy of the chase. You might think that actual long-term relationships are unthinkably boring. What on earth can you do after all that fun is over?

I'll tell you, firsthand. Yep, I have Mars in Aries. I enjoyed dating, I enjoyed being pursued, and on occasion I enjoyed being the pursuer. I didn't have to be in a relationship all the time, for Mars in Aries likes independence, but when I was with someone, I made sure it was interesting. While I had stable relationships, I always had a nervous feeling that one day there would be nothing to talk about, nothing to experience. I had a buried, subtle dread of boredom. This is the dark side of Mars in Aries, the fear that challenge and excitement will fade over time.

Well, here's the punch line. Life is going to be filled with so many different challenges and ambitions, and commitment makes things easier. Once love is fulfilled (in a good long-term relationship), you're free to tackle other goals. That doesn't mean that you're headed for dullsville in your love life. Passion, flirtation, sexiness, mystery, allure—they all have their place and come back to the surface now and then. You only have to be patient and trusting. Okay, that's not easy, but that's the way it is.

Mars brings another little "beware" factor to the table. Mars in Aries likes to lead the charge and some women (me included) can get a little too masculine and competitive to allow romance to bloom. This in no way implies that you look like a guy. It's just that you can act like one (does being "one of the guys" sound familiar?). This, of course, diminishes your romantic allure. Mars in Aries just gravitates here naturally. In fact, women with Mars in Aries don't always think so much about boyfriends. Annie Oakley, the lead character in *Annie Get Your Gun*, must have Mars in Aries, since she sings, "Anything you can do, I can do better." That about sums it up.

Watch your push factor when you have Mars in Aries. You can push romance right out the window.

AstroBabe Planetary Pulse: 3
Aries Mars Guy Planetary Pulse: 3

Mars in Taurus

The great aggressive energy of Mars takes a breather when it hits the gentle, supportive land of Taurus. Instead of campaigning for new conquests and bracing for adventure, the warrior planet mellows out. It's not to say that this hardworking energy falls asleep; he simply changes gears. Challenges are faced calmly, situations are evaluated, and courses are plotted. Deeper consideration is given to every move. Sometimes Mars in Taurus can look a little slow off the mark, a little lazy, but don't be fooled. Something is going on beneath the surface.

Given the stable nature of Taurus and the calming influence it has on Mars, romantic adventures take a different spin. For AstroBabes, Mars in Taurus creates a great deal of expectation. Any guy who wants this girl is going to have to be pretty special. He has to be sweet and gentle. He has to really understand the word "sensual" and enjoy touching, stroking, and just cuddling. This guy has to be a good lover, of course, but making love is almost second to the foreplay and afterglow. AstroBabes with Mars in Taurus need a guy who is comfortable with just being together.

And what do AstroBabes with Mars in Taurus actually do to get this wonderful, sensual, passionate, caring, cool guy? Typically, nothing. Mars in Taurus can make a girl a little too low-key. Instead of beckoning him over with a little of that Taurus charm, she might have the idea that he's just going to arrive out of nowhere at her doorstep ready for a deeply connected relationship with her. Nuh-uh, girlie. Ain't gonna happen.

If you have Mars in Taurus, you must learn to make an effort. It doesn't take much, but you have to let him know you're there, and available. Don't expect to get what you want without trying. And don't be afraid to go after it. You won't find a whole lot of guys who do fit your needs, so when one comes along, don't let him slip away. Do as the song says, and "show him that you care."

P.S. If the guy you like has Mars in Taurus, he probably won't make the first move. You don't have to be *too* forward, but create the space for something to happen or it never will!

AstroBabe Planetary Pulse: 1
Taurus Mars Guy Planetary Pulse: 2

Mars in Gemini

Feisty Mars leaps into airy Gemini looking for action. What is there to know? What can I think about? What's new? Mars likes a challenge, a task, a purpose. Gemini loves ideas, thoughts, concepts, connections. Mars likes to confront, to argue. Gemini likes to think through problems, to solve, to ponder.

Put Mars in Gemini and you get a mind ready to embrace something new. We're talking curiosity, pal. AstroBabes with Mars in Gemini don't sit still if there's nothing interesting happening. The phrase "same old, same old" is your kiss of death. Forget steady, sure-as-he-goes types. You are not about to be pinned down.

For romance, this means a guy who is out there doing things. Okay, maybe he watches football on TV, but he also likes to get up and do stuff. Anything from playing sports to going to the theater— this guy has a lot of interests and so do you.

Of course, he also has to have a killer sense of humor. He has to be able to talk and articulate his feelings. But with your Mars in Gemini, he mostly has to keep you on your toes. You need to feel that he contributes to your world, to your mind, in some way.

It's not like he's got to be your teacher, but he has to have his own ideas and he won't mind sharing them or defending them. He also wants to hear what you have to say. Will you change his mind? That's not as important as simply sharing ideas and opinions.

AstroBabes with Mars in Gemini bore easily. Here's your challenge. Don't interpret a lull in conversation or a little quiet patch in a relationship to mean that it's over for you. You have to learn patience (never easy for any planet in Gemini) and you have to make your own fun sometimes. Your guy is not solely responsible for keeping you amused in life. Before you let an impulse lead you astray (remember that curiosity killed the cat!), take time to remember how much you have enjoyed each other in the past. Know that you'll have that again. It's called trust.

AstroBabe Planetary Pulse: 3
Gemini Mars Guy Planetary Pulse: 3

Mars in Cancer

When Mars the Warrior sits in Cancer the Crab, the result is not a peace-loving, at-ease energy. It's more like a sleeping grizzly bear; whoever wakes it up can get a nasty gash. Mars in Cancer brings a stealthy, sharp edge to an AstroBabe.

Your energy is bold, passionate, and independent. You're ambitious. You have confidence. That's terrific. But whatever or whoever stands in your way or interrupts you or breaks your concentration will find you to be, well, crabby. Yes, that's it. You can get pretty irritated with people and you don't mind showing it. Mars in Cancer isn't easygoing, soft, cuddly, and nurturing. Mars in Cancer is definitely sensitive and creative, but there's simply not a lot of tolerance for other people getting in your way.

In love, this moody, peevish part of you won't surface right away. You won't let on that you're a little demanding, a little sensitive or prickly. You won't even feel that way until you're comfortable in a relationship, and then, whammy! Whatever traits you've been showing off—your Sun, Moon, Mercury, or Venus—forget it. Once that Mars in Cancer is allowed out, it never goes back inside.

Don't worry about it. First of all, this is authentically you, and whoever loves you is going to accept this. Second, you don't have to be a slave to your temper. You can handle it. I suggest a physical activity that allows you to release your anger, like kickboxing or tennis. Hit that ball as hard as you feel like and you'll win a lot of sets.

The best thing you can do for yourself is allow your anger to surface. If you try to stuff it down, it only gets more irritated and more powerful. Although Cancer is the sign of the home and the mother, of nurturing and holding, Mars gets pretty cranky here. If you deny your temper, it will only get worse. That doesn't mean haul off and hit someone. Just acknowledge that you have a little fire inside and channel it into passion. That's the best place for contained energy to be released.

AstroBabe Planetary Pulse: 2
Cancer Mars Guy Planetary Pulse: 1

Mars in Leo

Fiery Mars in Sun-drenched Leo gives a powerful energy to AstroBabes. There is a fearlessness in love and passion that is unique to you, and lucky are those with whom you share it!

Mars mutes its warrior nature in Leo through the distraction of entertainment, sports, and all kinds of competitive games. Mars doesn't need to contain its energy in Leo, where any kind of physical exertion is encouraged. AstroBabes with Mars in Leo are enthusiastic players, and mostly good-natured competitors. You roll the dice and hope for the best. And if it's not a jackpot, you simply roll again.

When it comes to dating, Mars in Leo enjoys the chase, taking turns being the one who's hard to get. Frankly, as long as the game is played well, you enjoy it. You can give as good as you get. You like a little challenge as long as it's all for fun.

In love, Mars in Leo is ardent and, as already mentioned, physical. That means sex and passion. Sometimes you'll even surprise yourself with untapped abandon. You get better with age and you never have to slow down.

So, here's the other side of Mars in Leo. You can get easily carried away and demand too much attention. Of course you're sunny, active, and up for anything. You also like to be recognized and appreciated, as any good Leo would insist. AstroBabes with Mars in Leo like feedback—the attention and recognition you deserve. If you find yourself asking, "Did you see what I did?" more than once, you're leaning a little too heavily on your ability to fascinate. You're innocently thinking, "Isn't this cool? Did you catch that?" out of the desire to share your experience, but everyone else is thinking you're a high-maintenance ego freak (not a good look on you). Chances are you've been there, done that, and then felt misunderstood. Never fear—you let that kind of behavior get the better of you only when you're insecure. And how often is that?

Mars in Leo is an AstroBabe's asset. You live, love, and share your passion with generosity and joy.

AstroBabe Planetary Pulse: 4
Leo Mars Guy Planetary Pulse: 5

Mars in Virgo

The energy of Mars, with all of its force and can-do spirit, lands in the earth sign of Virgo and can't wait to get busy. Virgo's mutable energy and its ability to take on simultaneous projects makes for a play-ground for task-hungry Mars.

What does this mean for romance? You aren't scared of it, that's for sure. AstroBabes with Mars in Virgo are happy to give romance a shot as well as all the other things you've got on your list to conquer. Maybe calling romance a back-burner issue is putting it a little strongly, but you are pretty selective about who you go out with. Let's just say it's not on the top of your to-do list.

You're also not into quantity. While some Astro-Babes can date for a hobby, you can't be bothered with mass amounts of guys. You'd rather have one quality dude than a whole group of average Joes. Your friends might think you're hard to please. The guys you reject will think you demand too much. But you know inside when the right guy shows up.

If the darker side of this planetary placement isn't

yet apparent, here it is: you can be too critical. Not everyone has the stamina, intellect, and thirst for accomplishment that you do. The world is made up of all sorts of imperfect beings, you included. When you study your list of the qualities your guy must possess, be willing to let one or two go. Don't forget, opposites attract. You might find an Oscar for your Felix.

If you find a guy who is not afraid of your high standards (and maybe has a few of his own), see if you can overlook the fact that he has a weakness for Adam Sandler movies. I know it's hard, but try.

No matter who ends up melting your heart, you can be sure that no one will ever fulfill *all* of your criteria. And remember, the road to permanent romance is paved with almost-but-not-quite Mr. Rights, and you need to sample a few of those before you get to your keeper.

So put aside your list once in a while and devote that boundless energy to some fun with regular people. You won't regret the experience on the way to The One.

AstroBabe Planetary Pulse: 2
Virgo Mars Guy Planetary Pulse: 4

Mars in Libra

Fiery Mars, conflict-loving and looking for action, is an arrow without a cause in peace-loving Libra. In astrology, the placement of Mars in this sign is called its detriment. Its aggressive powers are weakened in the sign of Libra. In fact, Mars is so weak it can't undertake any direct attacks, and instead finds ways to deploy its force with stealth and secrecy.

AstroBabes with this placement do whatever they can to avoid conflict. You have such a huge discomfort with anger, direct action, and confrontation that you'll take a long, circuitous route to stay out of their way. Some would call this passive-aggressive. Others would say it's cowardly. Only you know that you simply don't want to hurt anyone. That's your basic motivation for lying low. Otherwise you might say something harsh. You can, when pressed, argue very well—extremely well. But you don't want to be the one who hurls harsh language out there any more than you want to be the one in the direct line of fire.

To avoid conflict, you might be inclined to do something convenient that seems okay and justifiable at the time. Do you talk behind someone's back instead of confronting her head-on? Do you stretch the truth to justify what you want instead of simply stating your desires? This is the weakness of Mars in Libra, and it never works in the long run. Somehow, you don't get away with it.

The lesson here is to be okay with what's true. Don't worry about justifying what you know or what you want. It's simply what is.

If you're angry, your first impulse will be to plot, manipulate, and tweak your hostility into some kind of "innocent" reaction. ("Oh, I didn't *realize* you wanted to go to *that* game, so I gave those tickets away!") All you get with that kind of behavior is counterattack. Instead, hoof it over to the gym and try a kickboxing class followed by yoga (get out the anger—then find your center). Let the poor guy go to his game and pay you back with something fabulous (you sweet, understanding AstroBabe).

AstroBabes with Mars in Libra must eventually find ways to let anger dissipate without passing judgment or doling out punishment. Love is about forgiveness, nor righteousness.

AstroBabe Planetary Pulse: 3
Libra Mars Guy Planetary Pulse: 2

Mars in Scorpio

Great, forceful Mars and deep, intense Scorpio? That's a recipe for never-a-dull-moment. AstroBabes with Mars in Scorpio have great fires within, and the sign of Scorpio provides an almost volcanic playground for this energy to come forth. Will it stay beneath the surface or bubble up occasionally? Or will the force of Mars explode one day and annihilate us all?

Mars in Scorpio is first and foremost a very productive energy. AstroBabes with Mars in Scorpio are not slackers. You take in a lot of information and see opportunities that others miss. You know how to focus and use the information to achieve your goals. You're not easily intimidated, either, and perceptive people who sense your Mars energy don't take you on lightly. Your power paves the way to great accomplishments. —

Of course you have to get over the dark side, too. Since Mars is strong and combative and Scorpio is incisive and extreme, this combination is probably the most powerful in the zodiac. Scorpio uses focus and intuition to find the most vulnerable spot of an opponent; then Mars clobbers it. Expressed in words, your power can reduce someone to tears; expressed physically, it can be dangerous. Best to turn that Mars energy toward sports or physical work so that anger doesn't use it for something you'll regret. Also beware of turning the anger inward and getting into self-punishment—not very helpful in pursuing romance. And a guy with Mars in Scorpio is basically a big red flag—wait and see how he handles anger so you don't find out the hard way.

Mars in Scorpio does become very agreeable when there's a good time to be had: flirtation, parties, dinner out, any kind of social sport that offers the potential for passion or simply a good challenge. You hate to be bored.

If you take time to find the spiritual side of Mars in Scorpio, you will use that wonderfully deep power to make this world (and your life) a better place. There will be moments in your life when you will face a choice either to heal and be free from your pent-up anger or to be a servant to it. Take one of those opportunities to let go and believe in the greater good. Once you do, you won't suffer from internal anger and you won't let your hostility (an unattractive trait) be a barrier to deeply committed love.

AstroBabe Planetary Pulse: 4
Scorpio Mars Guy Planetary Pulse: 2

Mars in Sagittarius

Mars in any fire sign is a happy camper, and this placement for the planet of get-up-and-go is an easy fit. Fearless, adventurous, highly charged, the energy of Mars in Sagittarius makes an AstroBabe ready for fun.

Since Sagittarius is a mutable sign, Mars likes to switch gears, change direction, and try something new when it's inspired. For AstroBabes, this can be hard on the attention span. You love to roam, to experience, to challenge yourself, and you can get so caught up in your own interests that you forget about everything else. For some AstroBabes, the adventures will come in the great outdoors, with sports, exploration, and travel for hiking, skiing, or other activities. For other AstroBabes, thrills will be more cerebral, where learning about new ideas, philosophies, or cultures is as stimulating as a bungee jump. Whatever tack you take, you do so with dedication and integrity.

As far as the darker or more challenging aspects of Mars in Sagittarius, look no farther than your own tongue. You can't help but tell the truth, no matter how much it might hurt others. What you learn and your integrity are tantamount to who you are. So you can't let anyone leave with the wrong impression. Riding roughshod over other people's feelings is pretty much a Sagittarian trait, and Mars only makes it rougher. Learn to think before you share your opinion and you won't have that "What did I say?!" moment afterward.

As far as romance goes, the AstroBabe with Mars in Sagittarius is generally lucky in love. Lucky, that is, if the guy is able to handle your independent spirit, your need to follow your instincts and interests, and your very truthful way of saying what you think. No controlling types for you, no soft introverts—not even a low-key kind of guy is going to keep you interested for long. You need a confident, "let's go" kind of guy who will be happy to hold your hand on a hike and be equally as comfortable and trusting letting you go it alone.

You AstroBabes with Mars in Sagittarius are never alone for long, and are faithful to the core when the right one takes his place beside you.

AstroBabe Planetary Pulse: 4
Sagittarius Mars Guy Planetary Pulse: 4

Mars in Capricorn

There is a nice, mutually beneficial relationship between forceful Mars and ambitious Capricorn. Mars cannot get restless for lack of challenge, and Capricorn's desire to attain goals feeds the fire. Earth and fire get on very well together here.

Of course, the focus with Mars is on conquering. AstroBabes with Mars in Capricorn are intent on their goals. Most often those goals are real-world, get-it-done objectives. You're busy, that's for sure. AstroBabes with Mars in Capricorn work hard, play hard, and like to win. You don't shirk responsibility and happily take on positions of authority. You learn and guide yourself with intuition, but you are also patient enough to learn from others what you need to know. Slow but sure, that's Mars in Capricorn.

In romance, you can't help applying the same patience and fortitude to your desire for love. You have a worthy person in mind, someone who is your equal or at least close to it. You keep your emotions to yourself until you feel comfortable and you're certain they will be received with the right reaction. You focus your energy on one guy and slowly warm him, not burn him, with the fires of your passion. You certainly have the ability to love deeply, but you don't want it to take you away from your work and your other goals.

This is the tougher side of Mars in Capricorn. AstroBabes with this Mars can be distracted by professional ambition. It's not that love isn't important, but it's not a goal. You don't have time for socializing unless it's a step toward realizing your ambitions.

You do meet guys, of course, and sometimes they do interest you, but they have to really be worth knowing for you to give them your precious time and attention.

So you'll wait, bloom slowly, live your already full life until a guy who keeps you interested shows up. He'll be smart, maybe older, definitely patient, and he'll appreciate your desire to work. You'll begin to trust him and then, happily, allow love to enter your life. You're a faithful and loyal lover and you can probably say it ends with "happily ever after."

AstroBabe Planetary Pulse: 3
Capricorn Mars Guy Planetary Pulse: 4

Mars in Aquarius

Feisty Mars in airy Aquarius makes a fine combination of energy and expansiveness. In the realm of the intellect, Mars plays with knowledge and spars with words. Mars here makes for a great mind, forceful opinions, and an excellent ability to debate. Astro-Babes with Mars in Aquarius don't go for dummies.

Inventive, impulsive Aquarius is great for Mars energy. AstroBabe, you're the original creative mind, the groundbreaker, the seeker of new experiences and ideas, the fearless pioneer. You care about people and may take on the role of advocate for those who can't take care of themselves. You loathe social injustice and speak up against authority. In short, you're the type who saves the world, an intellectual superhero.

In romance, you're a verbal jouster. Don't try to participate in or enjoy superficial conversation about popular culture. Yes, you can do it, but you'll be bored later and you won't meet anyone who is worth knowing for long. You want to talk to someone who has something to say, and you want to be able to be serious when you feel like it. Anyway, when you don't care for the chat around you, your company knows it. You have standards that can be perceived as intellectual snobbishness.

The best part of love for you is a fierce and

passionate conversation or argument where you can feel your connection through both hearts and minds. Your ideal guy will be smart, able to take you on, and mesmerized by your wit, charm, and intelligence. You will not be happy with a shallow pretty boy, even if you *really* want him. Enduring relationships must have a strong and deep connection through ideas, ideals, principles, and values.

AstroBabes with Mars in Aquarius are inventive and unique and like their guys to be that way, too. Your natural resilience is strong; try to remember that some guys are more sensitive. While you can come and go, switch from hot to cold without a problem, you might be treading on someone's feelings. Turn around sometimes to see if you stepped on someone else. Your guy might be smart, strong, passionate, and tough, but he has a tender side you don't want to bruise.

AstroBabe Planetary Pulse: 1
Aquarius Mars Guy Planetary Pulse: 2

Mars in Pisces

What do you get when the warrior of Mars charges into the deep seas of Pisces? Roiling waters, strong currents, and warm pools. Mars cannot find a con-centrated force in this mutable water sign. And Pisces cannot completely dissolve the strength and heat of Mars' nature. The two strike up an uneasy relationship of directed energy and free-flowing creativity.

AstroBabes with Mars in Pisces are deeply sensi-tive and have strong feelings. Are you articulate? Probably not. Mars in Pisces can't directly approach uncomfortable territory. It's easier to swim or push around it, taking no more than little pokes and prods at your subject.

Guys can find you very provocative, puzzling, and even flirtatious, but it's not because you try to be that way. You shift away from things more often than you strategically approach new situations. It's not that you're afraid, but you don't want to be in a position to hurt someone else or to get hurt. Little white lies are common and big white lies that turn into monstrous dramas are not unusual for Mars in Pisces.

You now know your weaker side. Your wish that the waters always be smooth is simply not possible, and by trying to avoid problems in one place, you simply create them in another. You might start a fight about something totally different out of the desire to avoid what's really bothering you. You'll probably need to learn this the hard way, but believe me, though it's not easy to face the tough stuff head-on, it gets the job done a whole lot faster!

AstroBabes with Mars in Pisces are also grudge holders. You can't help it—you simply have a great memory and it's hard to let go of the wrongs done to you. It gets easier, though. When you realize that you hurt others, too (!), you'll be easier on those who hurt you.

In romance, Mars in Pisces gives you a lot of passionate energy. You are a great cuddler. You love to love, to have, to hold. It may take you some time to find that guy who is absolutely the right one for you, but he's there. Listen to your heart, not anyone else, and you'll make a good match.

AstroBabe Planetary Pulse: 3
Pisces Mars Guy Planetary Pulse: 3

SEVEN

AstroAssociations

At this point, you've become familiar with the planets and what they represent, you've worked out your personal planetary powers, and you have the ability to scope out a guy's Planetary Pulse. You've learned so much—congratulations! Now we can put it all together and go to the next level.

Stars Crossed or Stars Aligned?

It's not unusual for you to get confused about synthesizing all this—so don't panic! Maybe you're a mix of fixed, cardinal, and mutable, and a blend of fire, earth, air, and water. Or maybe you're one of those who do have a preponderance of one kind of energy—or a whole cluster of planets in the same sign. There is no good or bad. In every chart, there are gifts and challenges.

A Little Insight

In some cases, the alignment of the Sun and the Moon will give you additional information and add to understanding your AstroBabe powers. Since you know now that the Sun is the sign of your basic nature and the Moon is the ruler of your emotions, it's helpful to know how they work together.

Aspects of the Sun and the Moon

IF YOUR SUN AND MOON
SIGNS ARE THE SAME
You were born on a new moon. You are very connected to the moon and its phases. Since the new

moon is a great time for initiating new things, you might act more spontaneously than others. You are at ease with your feelings and you can use your intuition without much effort in all of your relationships.

IF YOUR SUN AND MOON ARE IN OPPOSITE SIGNS[1]

Your emotions and your sense of self are opposing each other. Most likely, you won't hold much stock in how you feel and prefer rational, practical reality to internal musings.

IF YOUR SUN AND MOON SIGNS ARE DIFFERENT BUT BOTH HAVE THE SAME ENERGY (BOTH CARDINAL, BOTH FIXED, BOTH MUTABLE)

You have a lot of that energy, for better or worse. Be on the lookout for the downside—for the fixed that means being stubborn, for the cardinal that means pushing your own agenda for better or worse, and

[1] Aries-Libra, Taurus-Scorpio, Gemini-Sagittarius, Cancer-Capricorn, Leo-Aquarius, Virgo-Pisces.

for the mutable that means not having the patience to stick to your plan. You can be your own worst enemy (if you're honest with yourself, you're nodding along in agreement). It's a lifelong challenge, but there it is. Resist falling into your own traps and you will be a winner.

IF YOUR SUN AND MOON ARE IN DIFFERENT SIGNS BUT THE SAME ELEMENT

You're pretty comfortable with yourself and you get along easily with others in that element. For instance, earth people simply understand each other on a practical level. Air people converse with ease. Fire people exhibit enthusiasm and a willingness to take on challenges. Water people feel each other out and get along with mutual quiet respect. To keep things interesting, beware of sticking with a crowd that is too watery, too earthy, too airy, or too fiery. You bring the knowledge and gifts of your element to the world, so share them with others.

Clashes or Smashes?

If you're worried about having a great basket of planets that don't seem to go together, worry not! Having a mix of energies and elements is a great way to be open to lots of different people. You won't rest too heavily on the energy or gifts of one sign; you'll blend and shift to use what works best for you. Pay attention first to your Sun and Moon signs, because they are likely to take precedence over Mercury, Venus, and Mars. If you find that you're attracted to lots of guys and they're all different, you're simply exploring the various opportunities open to you in your stars. Don't judge yourself based on consistency. Typically, the guy you don't notice at first ends up being someone special.

Who Is Mr. Right?

It's important to remember that there is no "right" answer. The guy you end up with might be a perfect star alliance or someone who is, on paper, an astrological anomaly. Your choice in love is ultimately up to you. Some partners are like two peas in a pod. Others, like me and my husband, are a marriage of opposites. As an AstroBabe, you are fully vested with personal celestial knowledge. You know all about your OWN strengths and weaknesses and have control over your choices. When you fall in love, enjoy the mystery of it. Use your Astro-Babe knowledge to understand your guy (and yourself) so that you can explore this relationship with integrity—and fun!

Personal Planetary Pulse: Expectation and Fulfillment

Your romantic expectations, your focus, and your comfort level are important to making romance successful. If you're lost in the clouds about perfect, endless love, you're not going to be happy with a guy who thinks romance is renting a horror flick and letting you choose the toppings for the pizza. And if you're an AstroBabe who isn't comfortable with hearts and flowers, you're not going to be cool with a weepy Romeo who serenades you with love songs. It doesn't mean the romance can't work. You just have to do two things: communicate your wants and needs, and resist pushing a good romantic prospect away because he doesn't seem to "get" you. There's a lot of wiggle room when it comes to flirtation, dating, and love.

A Personal Planetary Pulse is NOT a rating of your appeal. This number has nothing to do with your beauty or charisma or ability to attract a guy. It's not about getting a high number or a perfect 10. What tends to work best is a match of ranges. If you're in the low range and he's in the low range, great—you're not going to be disappointed. If you're in the high range, meaning your romantic ideals are strong, it's best to be with either someone who doesn't mind (and caters to) your desires, or a guy who is just like you. Some relationships never have a chance because you don't speak the same romantic language. Using the Personal Planetary Pulse will give you an idea of your desires and whether a certain guy is capable of fulfilling them.

Most Personal Planetary Pulse ratings are going to fall between 10 and 20. It's like a bell curve, where the very lowest and the very highest are the smallest populations. Chances are, you already have a hunch about your own rating. Given your guy's planets, you can see where he's coming from, too.

Add up your Planetary Pulse ratings after each summary. Here are mine (full disclosure).

Gemini Sun	2
Aries Moon	2
Cancer Mercury	1
Gemini Venus	2
Aries Mars	3
Total	10

It was no surprise to me that I had a medium-low romantic pulse. My love life has always been one interesting aspect of my life, along with my career, friends, and family. It's in balance, but still a very important element. My husband rates an 11, so we are happily compatible on that front!

The total pulse is going to be a guide to your romantic expectations and, if you have your love object's number, what he's capable of doing, as well. You might be surprised to know that some guys are really warm, romantic, idealistic lovers.

When you go on to read about your Personal Planetary Pulse, don't harbor that antiquated notion that bigger is better. If your pulse is high, it simply means you are a deeply committed romantic and you'd probably be better off with someone who can handle that. If you are more the "live in the real world" type, love will be more of an everyday thing, a nice part of your life that adds to but does not rule your entire happiness.

RATINGS

5–10

You are not the girl who dreamed of her wedding from the age of four. You are not the girl who dreamed of being swept off by Prince Charming. You are a self-possessed, smart, interesting person who is open to love but not obsessed by it. You have a great life, lots of energy, and lots to do. When a guy comes along who turns your head, you're definitely interested, but when your head returns to its original position, you're over it. Romantic notions don't fill your brain at the expense of everything else in your life. And this won't change much. You're going to fall in love, and you'll even get married (if you want to), but your wedding won't be the single most important day in your life. There are many important days for you, not just one.

If you meet a guy who has a high Planetary Pulse, he's going to go crazy trying to find a way to impress you. You have to give him a little feedback, as in "You're so sweet" or "How thoughtful of you." You won't find it easy all the time, but being polite and appreciative is important. He'll start to understand that you're not a "kittens in a basket" greeting card type and maybe he'll get you a gift certificate next time. If he's really important to you, permit him to express *his* notions of romance, even if it feels weird to you.

Naturally, you're going to feel more comfortable with someone who puts less emphasis on the mushy stuff. A guy with a Personal Planetary Pulse under

15 won't be too far out of your realm, but you'll have to work a little bit to keep your end of the romantic energy up. No forgetting birthdays or anniversaries, and remember, a few sweet words go a long way. Unless you have a guy with a pulse similar to yours, you're going to have to pick up on some cues. You don't have to act inauthentically, but you do have to try to dish out the sweet stuff when you know it means a lot.

11–15

You're not an all-work AstroBabe, but you have a short attention span for things in life that don't serve some purpose. Romance is great, in its place, but your happiness is fulfilled by your work, friends, family, and personal interests. If you had to balance romantic love and other interests, the scales would tip to those other things.

This isn't to say that you don't have the occasional dreamy moment, those phases when love swoops down on you and you lose your balance. Of course you're going to indulge in those pleasures with your full attention. You know how to flirt, you're good at socializing, and you know how to get out there and meet someone when the mood strikes you. But don't force it. You cannot and will not be goaded into romance unless it's something real and worthwhile.

In dating, you're the easygoing AstroBabe. If there's a guy in your life, he's meant to be there. If there's no one, you've got other things to do. You can take it or leave it.

It gets interesting when you meet a guy whose pulse lies at one of the extremes—low or high. If he's got a low Planetary Pulse, you'll wonder if he's actually into you at all. He might be fascinating, engaging, and mesmerizing because of his fabulous eyes or amazing smile, but his signals will be mixed. Is he just your friend or does he want more? Chances are, you're going to have to take the initiative to find out. The truth is, you won't want to take that step unless you know he's worth it, and, well, how will you know unless you try? AstroBabes with your moderate level of interest typically need a guy who is either near your pulse or only a tick above you on the scale. Coupled with a low-pulse guy, you're going to be platonic for a long, long time.

The other extreme, the guy with a very high

Planetary Pulse, is a goofball. He's soft, sweet, adoring, imaginative, and completely indulgent in love with all the trimmings. With him, you could feel put on the spot. Sometimes you're going to like it, but other times you may find yourself more embarrassed than flattered by his attentions and even his expectations. He will assume that you're a romantic, too. Depending on your level of interest and your patience, you could be—but not forever. Tread carefully with a high Personal Planetary Pulse. You'll think he's a hopeless romantic.

_16–20_

You're definitely a romantic. No doubt about it, you like to look for love, find love, be in love, and keep love going. Boyfriends were important at an early age. And if you have your way, romance will be an active and important part of your life all through the years.

This isn't to say that you don't have an interest in other things. Indeed, you can be gripped by your work, friends, and outside interests, so you look, at least to the outside world, like a normal, balanced person. You _are_ fairly balanced, but inside of you there is a little more to your "lovescape" than you let on.

You are great at flirting, dating, and being in love. You're even good at relationships, as long as the guy is willing to keep up the whole romantic theme. Once your guy falls short of your expectations, trouble starts. You need to give him gentle guidance (he doesn't always have to cough up violins and rose petals, just a little sign that he cares), but if he's more interested in the TV listings than your engaging smile, you're not going to be happy.

Romantic expectations can be your downfall. You will almost always be happy at the beginning of a relationship, when typically he tries his hardest to win you. The grim reality is that once you are won, he thinks he doesn't have to try so hard. But you still want some effort once in a while and you have to find a guy who's willing to dish it out.

For that reason you know that a guy with a low Personal Planetary Pulse is not going to keep you interested for long. He won't understand your need for attention or your desire to be playful. He might be sexually passionate, but he won't feel inclined to create romantic moments with you. You might just fall for him in the beginning, especially if you like a challenge (who can resist the cool, hard-to-get guy?). But you won't stay interested for long.

The easiest match for you is going to be a guy in your Personal Planetary Pulse range. If you hook up with a guy who has an appreciation for love and all its elements—music, candlelight, love letters, surprises, whatever it is—you'll be whisked into bliss. Guys who have their own sense of passion and play are going to be easy for you to love and to stay with.

With a guy whose Personal Planetary Pulse is even higher than yours, you'll be in awe and even a little thrown off kilter. He won't be as practical as you are and might just take love to limits you're not prepared to meet. Go easy on him and observe how he responds to your comfort level. If he's *too* out there, throw him back.

21–24

Welcome to the outer limits. Your Personal Planetary Pulse is tuned in to a level of bliss that can be achieved only by extraordinary means. You're dreamy, delightful, imaginative, idealistic. Just thinking about love fills you with happiness. Romance is a necessary part of your daily diet.

There aren't many people who can live up to your ideals, though. Romantic love is imperfect and bliss is a fleeting feeling. Keeping your feet on the ground is not your strength, and staying put in less-than-lovely circumstances is tough. Although you can heal and plant happiness in most any circumstance, your satisfaction and fulfillment will come and go just like it does for the rest of us mortals.

You possess the rose-colored glasses of love. You will see potential when your heart tells you to, even if your head is saying, "No way!" Few people will accuse you of being practical, and you'd be the first person to volunteer that your fantasy life is a lot better than what's on TV.

So where does this get you? In your youth, disappointment. Young AstroBabes will enjoy the path of love and learn the links to reality by falling in love, then waking up to real life—nothing's perfect! When you're older, you'll understand that life simply cannot live up to your ideals, so you'll make the most of a love relationship, flawed as it may be.

Maturity means separating fact from fantasy, resisting leaving a relationship because it's lost its luster or because your romantic dreams aren't coming true every Saturday night. Romance comes in many ways and in many layers, and though your high Personal Planetary Pulse demands that love is front and center, you'll learn that bliss rests just beneath the surface of everyday life.

A guy with a low Planetary Pulse is going to drive you nuts. It would be hard for you to even date a guy like that. You'll be hard-pressed for conversation and even more at a loss for flirtatious behavior. But at some point you'll fall for someone like this, probably at work, and you'll talk yourself into it because you'll see his potential (until you realize you were completely mistaken). It takes only one experience like this for you to learn that lesson, so 'nough said.

Guys with pulses in the middle range are going to be more in your league. Eventually you'll realize that the picnic-at-sunset phase is fading, and you'll be left with dinner in front of the TV. If he can summon his romantic pulse often enough for you to keep interested, you have a possible keeper. But if he's the dude who thinks chocolates on Valentine's

Day and a dinner out on your birthday is going to suffice, he'll get the boot.

Obviously, you're going to crave a guy who can match your own desire for love, bliss, romance, and passion. Frankly, it's not your best option. Can you imagine two of you spending all your time making each other happy at the expense of everything else in life? What about work, friends, children? To have a well-balanced life, one of you needs to keep your feet on the ground. Two people with a high Planetary Pulse are pleasure-seekers, perhaps at the expense of all else. As much as it might pain you, better share your high pulse with someone who isn't quite as gifted in that area. That way your feet might touch the ground once in a while and he just might get the hang of being a champion of romance.

SUMMARY OF PLANETARY PULSE POINTS

1. No-nonsense. Mating without much romance—a bit primitive.
2. Capable. There's room for a little deeply felt expression, once in a blue moon.

3. Adaptable. Romance is one of many interests—it works when it's right.
4. Absorbed. No romantic opportunity will go unexplored.
5. Adrift. Hopeless. Romance and love are everywhere—even where they shouldn't be.

1-No-nonsense 2-Capable 3-Adaptable 4-Absorbed 5-Adrift

Sun	Women	Men
Aries	1	4
Taurus	3	4
Gemini	2	1
Cancer	3	2
Leo	4	4
Virgo	2	3
Libra	4	5
Scorpio	4	4
Sagittarius	3	3
Capricorn	2	4
Aquarius	1	1
Pisces	5	3

1-No-nonsense   2-Capable   3-Adaptable   4-Absorbed
5-Adrift

Moon	Women	Men
Aries	2	3
Taurus	4	4
Gemini	3	2
Cancer	2	2
Leo	4	5
Virgo	3	2
Libra	5	4
Scorpio	1	1
Sagittarius	3	4
Capricorn	3	3
Aquarius	1	2
Pisces	4	3

1-No-nonsense   2-Capable   3-Adaptable   4-Absorbed
5-Adrift

Mercury	Women	Men
Aries	1	3
Taurus	4	2
Gemini	5	4
Cancer	1	1
Leo	2	3
Virgo	4	5
Libra	2	4
Scorpio	1	1
Sagittarius	3	2
Capricorn	3	3
Aquarius	4	4
Pisces	4	2

AstroBabe

1-No-nonsense 2-Capable 3-Adaptable 4-Absorbed
5-Adrift

Venus	Women	Men
Aries	1	2
Taurus	5	4
Gemini	2	2
Cancer	3	4
Leo	4	4
Virgo	2	3
Libra	5	5
Scorpio	3	3
Sagittarius	3	3
Capricorn	3	3
Aquarius	3	2
Pisces	5	3

1-No-nonsense 2-Capable 3-Adaptable 4-Absorbed
5-Adrift

Mars	Women	Men
Aries	3	3
Taurus	1	2
Gemini	3	3
Cancer	2	1
Leo	4	5
Virgo	2	4
Libra	3	2
Scorpio	4	2
Sagittarius	4	4
Capricorn	3	4
Aquarius	1	2
Pisces	3	3

The Happy Ending

It's up to you to be a fully empowered AstroBabe.
This knowledge will never leave you and will be
useful for the rest of your life. You are in charge of

your own happiness, and you now have the power to create it.

AstroBabes know that love doesn't necessarily mean only deeply shared moments of tenderness. Although all good relationships have some of those, passion can be fueled by so much more.

If AstroBabes do anything, it's busting the myth of what makes love work. We make it work with our passion, our creativity, our stubbornness, and our weaknesses. Love is imperfect, thank goodness, so we can all enjoy it in the way that suits us best.

Love is a joy and a gift in this world. It's not something to achieve for the sake of being married. It's not a badge to wear or an item to be checked off on a list of what to accomplish in life. Love is a special connection that makes your life bigger. It fulfills you and encourages you to be all you can be.

Being an AstroBabe gives you more tools to make the love that comes to you flourish. Being an Astro-Babe enables you to draw from your many gifts and diminish the common pitfalls we all encounter from time to time. You are empowered. You are strong.

Now live your romance, passion, and love with all your AstroBabe glory.

Barrie Dolnick is a former Madison Avenue advertising executive and the author of the Simple Spells book series. She is also a high-profile consultant whose company, Executive Mystic, uses alternative information techniques, including tarot cards, astrology, meditation, and spell casting to guide clients on a successful path. For more information, log on to www.BarrieDolnick.com.